Califor...

by Angela Britnell

In Search Of Peace

I DON'T know, dear." Suzie Reynolds
sighed down the phone. "The Treneagues
are always saying we should visit, but
people do that and don't really expect you
to turn up on their doorstep. Why don't you
look for another job there?"

"Mom." Christa used the wheedling tone
that always annoyed her mother, but nine
times out of ten achieved her purpose.
"Nana always said I should go. You
promised her you would, too, one day, so
why don't you come with me?"

She instantly wanted to bite off her
tongue. If a woman chose to run away from
her life she shouldn't take her mother along.

In the last six months she'd been moved
to the dreary social events section of the
newspaper, been jilted by her fiancé, and

then this morning her hair stylist convinced her some colour would enhance her natural beauty. Her harmless blonde shoulder-length locks were now about three inches long all over with a red streak down the middle.

The final straw came after lunch when her new editor handed over the information about the couple to be featured in her "Wedding Of The Week" column. She'd frozen at the sight of a photo of Antony Horwath with his arm wrapped around a delicate blonde enveloped in yards of lace and tulle. She'd scanned over the details of the ceremony and read the detailed description of the elaborate wedding.

Knowing Antony was getting married and having her nose rubbed in it were two very different things. She was supposed to interview the couple, but pleaded with her editor to be saved from any more humiliation. Naturally he'd told her to do her job or he'd find someone else to do it for her. She'd quit before he could fire her.

Christa became aware her mother was still speaking.

"Now you're being ridiculous. Who'd look after your father? He'd never manage for five minutes on his own," Suzie insisted. "I'll give you their number but don't assume they'll want you for more than a few nights."

"Thanks, Mom, you're the best. Couldn't I

fire off an e-mail instead of phoning?"

Suzie's laugh resonated down the line.

"Cornwall's the most remote part of England. I'm sure they have internet connections there but I'm pretty certain the Treneagues don't at home."

"OK, I'll be home tomorrow so we'll sort it out then." Christa hung up before her mother could ask any more questions.

For a moment she wondered if she was doing the right thing. Nearly 70 years ago her English-born grandmother was evacuated from war-torn London to safety in Cornwall. She'd keep her fingers crossed the same family would help in her own search for a different sort of peace.

***

Piles of clothes lay strewn over the bed as Christa conducted her rather haphazard version of packing. She struggled to focus on whether to take a thin rain jacket or a warmer coat, instead of dwelling on Antony and his new bride. Had he any clue how much he'd hurt her? And to submit his wedding picture, knowing she'd be the one writing about it, was beyond cruel.

As tears slid down her cheeks, Christa slumped down on to the bed and clutched her knees tightly to her chest. After a few minutes she sniffed, blew her nose, and jumped back up. Feeling sorry for herself was a waste of time and she refused to be the sort of woman she'd sworn never to be.

An hour later she had her case packed, the fridge cleaned, and she was ready. She couldn't bear to wait until tomorrow and it would only take her about five hours to drive the 300 or so miles from Los Angeles up the coast to Monterey. She flipped open her cell phone and told her parents she was on the way.

****

Christa drove slowly along the last few streets before home, past the playground where her four older brothers used to torment her, and finally arrived at the house. Grabbing her small overnight bag she breezed in and flung open the kitchen door.

"I'm here!"

Two shocked faces stared at her in disbelief. Christa had forgotten all about her hair.

****

Gatwick Airport was a zoo but Christa pushed through the crowd and grabbed her suitcase from the slow-moving airport carousel. When she'd finally spotted her purple case with its big sunflower stickers she'd allowed herself to breathe again.

It was hard to believe she was in London only three days after calling Mary Treneague, but she'd been encouraged to come as soon as possible. First she needed to catch the train to Reading and then connect with the main line out of London heading down to Cornwall. She set off for the last part of the long journey.

Christa hadn't bargained on the largely unintelligible accents of everyone she spoke to – the notion they all spoke the same language was plainly false. There was American English and British English and the two appeared to bear little resemblance.

The strange money made no sense either – she suspected things were wickedly expensive but was too tired to care. Finally she made it and fell into an empty seat at Reading. Over the next few hours she managed a couple of brief naps and risked a thin, dry sandwich from the buffet car, totally understanding why most people brought their own.

She recalled Mary encouraging her to pay attention when the train crossed the Tamar River into Cornwall, but slept right through it, only just managing in her jet-lagged haze to catch the name of the station before hers. She stood up and stretched her aching arms before heading off to freshen up.

Christa hauled her case and carry-on bag over to the door and watched the lush, green countryside speed by. The train came to a noisy halt and she barely managed to unlock the door and haul her luggage on to the platform before it pulled away again.

She breathed heavily and looked around. The neat station with its hanging baskets full of colourful flowers and freshly painted benches cheered her, and for the first time since she got on the plane in California she decided this trip might not be a bad idea.

Getting To Know You

YOU must be Christa Reynolds."

A deep, male voice interrupted her reverie and she stared at the tall man standing a few steps away.

"And why would you assume that?"

His dark eyes flashed with a touch of humour and she almost smiled back but wasn't in the mood.

"You're the only female getting off at this stop with nobody meeting them, and when you yelled at the guard just now I heard an American accent."

Mary had explained her lodger would collect Christa, but she'd expected someone old and shabby with nowhere else to live but the spare room in someone else's house. This man, with his cut-glass accent and good looks, hardly fitted that description.

"The name's Dan Wilson, but if you want to be formal you can call me Captain Daniel Jonathan Wilson, Royal Marines, retired."

She should've guessed by the way he stood, very erect, feet spread slightly, with watchful eyes that missed nothing.

"That figures."

"Excuse me? What exactly do you mean?" His deep stare matched the measured tone of his voice.

A rush of heat flushed her skin.

"Only that you have the distinctive stance. They always say it's obvious when someone's been in the military."

Dan raised one eyebrow.

"Really."

"Yes, really. Now could we get going, please? I've been up for twenty-four hours straight and I'm exhausted."

"Of course, I'm sorry. Just a warning before we get there – they've been preparing for you coming all week and you'll be waddling around in a day or two if you eat everything they've cooked."

"Thanks, I'll keep that in mind."

He picked up her bags and walked away, his left foot dragging with a pronounced limp and she rushed to help him.

"It's heavy, let me." Christa tried to grab her case but dropped her hand back to her side as Dan threw her a fierce scowl.

"It's a bad knee, that's all." He almost marched out through the station entrance and she followed at a discreet distance, standing back while he loaded her bags into an old blue Volvo.

"Jump in," he ordered and she did, crossing her fingers as he started up the car.

Christa gripped the side of the seat as Dan drove way too fast for someone on the wrong side of the road, although she personally wouldn't classify the narrow winding route as much better than a farm track. They rounded a sharp corner and Dan slammed on the brakes, inches from the front of a tractor.

"Having a good time yet?" Dan asked, a fleeting smile tugging at the corners of his stern mouth.

"Oh, just wonderful. Did Mary specify I had to be alive when you got me there?"

"I don't believe she did." Dan suddenly pulled off the road at the top of a steep hill and killed the engine. "Out you get."

"Why?"

"Mary said I had to stop and let you see Tremorva from here because the weather's good today." He gestured across at the clear blue sky and shimmering sea reaching out in front of them. "Make the most of it. It might not be like this again for another month."

"Cheerful, aren't you?"

He didn't answer, but got out and walked around to open her door, gesturing for her to follow him.

As they stood together Christa breathed in the fresh salty air and struggled to damp down her excitement. The rugged granite cliffs dropped down to a tiny village nestled around a harbour full of small fishing boats. Rows of pastel-coloured cottages dropped away from her view and she wondered about the people who lived there.

"Cat got your tongue?" he teased.

Christa gave a brief smile and dismissed the view with a careless shrug.

"Pretty enough, I guess. Can we go now?"

"Certainly."

There was almost a touch of sarcasm in his reply but she ignored it and got back into the car without another word.

Halfway down the steep hill they pulled into the driveway of a large old house, its faded white exterior and dark green paint worn by constant exposure to the sea air. The front door was instantly flung open and a short, dumpy woman filled the doorway, calling over her shoulder back into the house.

"Mum, she's here."

Before she had a chance to speak Christa was swept into a warm lavender and mothball-scented hug. The woman's pale blue eyes checked her out before her round, lightly wrinkled face creased into a welcoming smile.

"I'm Mary. You must be worn out, my 'andsome. Come on in. Mum's been some excited all week. She's had me dragging out all the old photos and telling all kinds of stories about what she and your gran used to get up to."

"Excuse me." Dan interrupted with a sharp nod. "I'll take Miss Reynolds' bags upstairs. I won't be in for tea." He stalked past them and out of sight.

Mary gave Christa a searching look.

"Did something upset our Dan?"

"I expect he's being thoughtful and leaving us to get to know each other." She wasn't sure it was true but he'd unsettled her and Christa was pretty sure the less time they spent together the better.

"I expect you're right. He's a good man but he's had a difficult time." Mary nodded.

"What happened to his leg?"

"I'm thinking he'll tell you if he wants." Mary looked serious for a moment and then her warm smile popped right back. "Whatever am I thinking leaving you out on the doorstep? Come in and we'll have us a proper cup of tea. From what I've heard they never feed you on those airplanes, and the trains are worse."

Christa wasn't about to disagree with that. She followed the older woman in through a hallway papered with dark red roses and trimmed in thick cream paint.

"Mum's over here in the front room." Mary opened a door on the right and led the way into a small, dimly lit room crowded with old-fashioned dark furniture. An old woman sat close to a small electric fire, turned on full blast against the damp chill of the mid-March afternoon.

"Come over here, my dear. I'm Granny Treneague, but you can call me Irene if you'd rather." Her wrinkled hand stroked down the side of Christa's face and for a second her pale blue eyes misted over. "You'm so like poor Bea, it's…"

Christa was speechless. She only knew of her grandmother from her mother's stories and the few photos remaining of a beautiful woman with laughing blue eyes and flaming red hair.

"Mother, are you coming over to the table tonight?" Mary asked kindly.

The small table over by the window was covered in a snowy white tablecloth, barely visible beneath plates of food and an enormous teapot – not exactly the drink

14

and a cookie Christa had expected. With a smile she remembered Dan's warning.

Irene huffed.

"Of course I am." She reached for the carved wooden cane by the side of her chair and gestured to Christa. "You can get my other arm, my dear."

As they made their way across the room Christa heard heavy footsteps on the stairs and the front door slammed. She turned back to concentrate on what Mary was saying, relieved to know she wouldn't have to face Dan again any time soon.

She started to eat what she suspected would be the first of many slices of cake.

****

Christa peered at the luminous figures on her bedside clock. Two o'clock. Surely having missed a night's sleep she should be exhausted? Her recent battle with insomnia must have sneaked in the suitcase and followed her 4,000 miles across the Atlantic Ocean. Unless she got up and tired herself out by reading or watching TV she'd stare at the ceiling until about six then fall into a stupor and wake up in a sleep-deprived fog about an hour later.

Slipping out of the bed she shivered and pulled on the blue sweater she'd travelled in

over her pyjamas. She found a pair of wool
socks and yanked them on along with a pair
of canvas shoes. She crept down the steep
stairs and hesitated at the living-room door.
It wouldn't endear her to her hosts if she
woke them in the middle of the night.

Christa sneaked out through the hall and
into the kitchen where a small night light
glowed over the stove. She crossed over to
the window and pulled back the flowery
curtains and gazed on to the small back
garden. Yesterday, when she'd called it a
cute yard, they'd all laughed at her in a kind
way. Apparently the word yard referred to
the area around a farm house, not this small
strip of grass surrounded by beds crammed
full of spring flowers.

She checked for a key but didn't see one
anywhere so cautiously tried the door
handle and it turned easily in her hand.
Didn't they have burglars in Cornwall?

The cold air hit her straight on, taking her
breath for a moment, but she refused to be
a wimp. Christa didn't intend to be labelled
a spoilt American. She made her way slowly
along the path snaking up through the
garden. Yesterday she'd noticed it curved
slightly to the right about halfway along
and her inherent curiosity made her want to
see what was there.

Drat! She should've stayed in bed.

"Don't worry, I won't bite. It's not a full moon." Dan sat on an old wooden bench in front of a dilapidated shed, grinning at her.

"Sorry, I didn't know anyone was…"

"I said it's all right and I meant it. Jet lag messes you up, doesn't it?"

"Yeah. It's colder than I thought, though. I'd better get back inside."

"Don't do that." Dan grabbed a sweater off the back of the bench and threw it over to her. "Here, put this on."

Christa pulled it over her head and let it drop all the way down past her slim hips. She sat next to Dan and studied the garden.

"Mary does all this when she's got time. I've been helping her and doing a few repairs around the house. Hopefully they don't feel I'm taking advantage."

"What do you mean? Why would you have to do anything?"

He gave her a questioning look.

"I assumed Mary would've told you."

"Told me what?"

His long well-shaped fingers fiddled with a hole in the knee of his jeans.

"Mary won't take any money because I'm her nephew."

"You're kidding? But you don't sound… local." Christa didn't want to admit she had problems understanding Mary and Irene Treneague's broad Cornish accents,whereas

Dan came across more like the BBC programmes she enjoyed watching.

"In a way I'm not. My mother, Lizzy, was Aunt Mary's younger sister. She left here at sixteen and headed for London." The warmth left his face. "She met my dad there and they got married."

He hesitated and glanced away from her before carrying on.

"Dad made sure I went to all the best schools, which explains the accent."

Christa knew this wasn't the whole story but was wary of asking too much.

"Where are your parents now?"

Dan sprung to his feet and grabbed a walking stick from the side of the bench.

"Gone." He stalked off.

She watched his difficult progress back through the garden and cursed herself for being tactless. Even through Dan's warm sweater she shook with the cold, but hung on for another five minutes before running back inside and up to bed.

That was the last she knew until nearly noon the next day.

****

"I thought you'd be glad of a cup of tea, dearie. It's a lovely day. You must've brought the good weather with you." Mary placed the tea on the bedside table and walked over to pull back the bright yellow curtains.

"There's a clean towel on your chair, so why don't you have a nice bath after you've had your tea and then come down for a bit of lunch." Mary bustled around and gave her a smile before scurrying out of the room.

Christa gathered up clean clothes and her wash things and found the bathroom. After her bath, she chose a clean pair of jeans and added a simple long-sleeved mint green shirt to help tone down her appearance.

"We're in the kitchen, love, come in." Mary shooed Christa over to sit down. "You'm looking peaky after all that travelling. A bit of fresh air will do you good after you've eaten. Dan's offered to take you to look around the village if you'd like."

"There's no need for him to bother. I'm sure I can find my own way down."

"Aunt Mary asked, and I said I'd be happy to," Dan interjected.

"There you go, your first Cornish pasty," Mary passed the plate across.

"Uh, thank you. Do you mind me asking what it is?" Christa prodded the large pie with her fork and Dan burst out laughing, unable to stop himself.

"Don't worry. There's only beef, potato, onion and turnip inside, not boiled eye of newt." He cut through the middle of his own and showed her. "They were originally made for the tin miners to take for their lunch and sometimes they'd have apple or jam in one half. Usually they didn't eat pastry on the end they were holding, in case they got arsenic on their hands from the mine, but you don't have to worry about that today."

"I'm sure it's delicious, but it's big enough to feed a whole family!" Christa exclaimed.

"I bet you finish it." Dan tossed her a challenging grin and began to eat his own.

Christa cautiously took her first bite and didn't say another word until it was gone.

"That was delicious!" she declared and pushed her empty plate away. "If you're ready we can go now."

"What about pudding? I've made a lovely sherry trifle." Mary frowned at Dan.

"I don't know about Christa, but I'm full and need to walk this off first." A touch of relief flitted across Christa's face and Dan felt pleased to have read her mind.

Christa jumped up and headed for the door with Dan following close behind.

Dan felt Mary and his gran's curiosity bore into the back of his neck and suddenly got the niggling suspicion he and Christa were being set up. If that was true they were wasting their time. He had enough problems in his life already.

A Shock For The Family

STOP here a minute, this is the best view." Dan leaned against the low granite wall and gazed out over the ice green sea. Here, the light varied from one hour to the next, the sky reflecting the weather as clearly as any television weather map.

A quick breath of Christa's light floral scent pulled his attention back to her.

"So, what made you suddenly decide to come to Cornwall? There's got to be more to it than wanting to see where your grandmother spent so much time."

A shadow crossed Christa's face and he guessed he'd put his foot in it.

"What does it matter? I think it'd be better if you let me explore on my own today."

"I'm sorry." He hesitated. "I seem to have forgotten how to talk to people."

The obvious hurt clouding her pretty blue eyes startled him.

"I'm sorry, honestly. Can we start again?" Dan rested a hand on her arm. "If we walk on down to the harbour we can get out of this wind and have some tea if you'd like."

"Does anyone here makes decent coffee instead?" she said with a mischievous grin.

"I might know somewhere, only don't tell

Aunt Mary I didn't treat you to a proper cream tea." He wagged a finger.

"The words cream and tea sound lethal together. I'd like to still fit into my jeans next week."

He'd been admiring her neat figure but stopped himself saying so just in time.

"Take me to this illicit coffee shop. I'm getting cold." She rubbed her hands together and shivered.

He searched in the pocket of his old green waxed jacket and pulled out a folded up waterproof, shaking it loose.

"Do you specialise in having clothes at the ready for needy females?" she teased.

"Just wear it." He sighed.

Christa grabbed the jacket and pulled it on, but her cold hands fumbled with the zipper so he pushed them out of the way and did it up himself. Their eyes met and there was an instant connection he hadn't experienced for a very long time.

"There you go," he murmured and she jerked out of his hold.

Christa strode away, faster than he could walk these days. He finally caught up with her at the quay. The tide was in and a multitude of small boats filled the harbour. Chalk boards were propped up around the place advertising deep sea fishing trips and sightseeing tours of the coastline. This early in the year there weren't any takers and most of the owners hung around idly passing the time.

"They make their living from tourists in the summer. The fishing's not up to much these days with too many EEC rules and foreign fishermen taking their catch."

Dan wanted her to see beyond the pretty scene that always entranced strangers.

"Most of the youngsters have to leave to get jobs and so many outsiders buy second homes there's not much left that's affordable."

"That's a shame."

"Things change even when we don't want them to. You're old enough to know that." He met her shrewd blue eyes and sensed understanding there. "Let's go and get some coffee."

Squeezed into a table by the window, Christa concentrated on the hot coffee and her earlier irritation drained away.

Dan finished his cup and pushed away from the table, absentmindedly straightening his left leg and rubbing at the knee. An athletic young couple jogged along the road in front of the window. Suddenly, Dan turned back to face Christa.

"You won't rest until someone tells you and Aunt Mary and my gran won't, so I suppose I have to."

"You don't owe me any explanations," Christa replied.

"I'm too sensitive. Maybe I'll grow out of it one day." He struggled to smile but it didn't go any further than the edges of his mouth. "I'd rather you know the truth. I was with the Royal Marines in Afghanistan and was involved in an incident."

Briefly, he closed his eyes and impulsively she reached across the table to touch his hand.

"I was injured pretty badly," he went on, "but they managed to save my leg, although it's not good for much. I was invalided out."

"Why are you staying here?" Christa probed, wanting to understand this intriguing man.

"I've got money and I'll get a job when I'm ready."

"You can't run away from life for ever." Christa stamped down on the thought that she was doing exactly the same.

"You only met me yesterday – why should you care?" His voice rose and the other customers stared their way. Christa gently squeezed his hand and lowered her voice.

"Why don't we head back? If you want my story in return, I'll explain…" It was the least she could say after being so rude.

Dan paid and they headed outside and

stood over by the railings. Noisy seagulls swooped down like vultures around the scraps left over from the morning's fish market and their raucous cries filled the air.

Dan's sharp eyes fixed on her.

"Let's leave any more stories for now and keep something for amusement when we're bored on a rainy day."

As she glanced up Dan leaned down slightly and rested one finger on her lips, then took it away with a small sigh. He started to walk away and Christa dared to slip her arm through his free one, absurdly pleased when he didn't protest.

After a slow, quiet walk back up the hill they approached the house, and as the front door opened Christa moved her hand back down to her side, catching the quick flash of Dan's smile.

"I'm some glad you're back. The postman brought this from Pat Carhart. It's the end." Mary stood waving a letter at them, her eyes wet with tears.

Dan wrapped a comforting arm around his aunt's shoulders.

"Don't upset yourself. Come on, it can't be that bad."

Mary gave Christa a weak smile.

"Did you have a nice time, my dear? I hope Dan took you to our place for tea."

Luckily for Christa, Dan interrupted.

"Not today. She wasn't hungry enough to do justice to one of your famous cream teas so I let her off."

"Don't tell me you took her to that other place? I know you go there, you wicked boy."

"I'm sorry, but it's all her fault. She hasn't an extra pound on her and is one of these modern women who want to keep it that way. I'll have to persuade her real men like something to grab hold of." He gave a sly wink in her direction and she couldn't resist smiling back.

"Come on, Auntie, let's go in. I bet you haven't told Christa about the café yet, have you?" He carried on when Mary didn't answer. "The Treneague family's had a business down in the village for years, the other side of the harbour from where we were, and…"

"Eighty-seven years, dearie." Mary interrupted. "My granny started a little shop and Mother changed it to a café for the tourists. Since she got poorly with the arthritis I've run it."

"Must be hard work and tough to make money in the wintertime."

"I've never been afraid of hard work and a couple of local girls help out when we're busy. Julie Tregargas is running things today so I could be here with you."

Dan steered his aunt towards the kitchen

and made her sit at the table while he busied himself putting the kettle on to boil. He poured a cup for his aunt, and slipped on a pair of square dark-rimmed glasses he retrieved from his inside jacket pocket.

He read the letter several times and the worry lines on his forehead deepened.

"Can he do that, Dan?" Mary's voice wavered.

"I'm not sure. Has anyone else received one?"

"I know Jenna and Robbie both have because they rang me."

Christa itched to find out what was going on, but felt it would be rude to ask.

"Our poor guest is wondering what on earth we're talking about. Do you want me to explain?" Dan patted his aunt's hand.

Mary turned to Christa.

"Oh, I'm some sorry, my love. I didn't mean to leave you out."

"No, please don't worry. It's family business. I'll leave you to talk."

Dan's warm chuckle took her by surprise.

"Don't be silly. You'll only listen at the door. Isn't that what nosy journalists do?"

She pretended to be offended but gave in to a grin. Her eyes met Dan's and her heart raced. Oh, boy, being attracted to him was the last thing she needed. He dragged his gaze away first and she sunk back in the chair with relief.

"Aunt Mary and the other shopkeepers along Bridge Street rent their shops from Pat Carhart. His family's owned them for generations and it's never been a problem until last year when Pat's father died and he immediately raised the rents. We'd heard rumours of developers wanting to buy up the whole area, pull it all down and build luxury flats, and this letter confirms it.

"Carhart's offering people a chance to buy him out, but he's asking an outrageous price. He's giving six months' notice that the leases will be terminated and is all set to make a killing. I don't think we can stop him." Dan tossed down the letter.

"So, you're giving up without a fight?" Christa heard herself say.

They all stared. The last time she went out on a limb and stirred up public outrage against the mayor's office she'd ended up covering weddings and tea parties. She never seemed to learn.

"What do you suggest?" Dan asked. "We rob a bank and steal the half a million pounds to buy the shop? There's a legal agreement, Christa, and unless a lawyer discovers a clause we don't know exists, the property is Carhart's to do with as he wishes."

"I'm sorry. I didn't mean to imply you didn't care." She quickly backtracked.

"Perhaps you can get the local people on your side, expose Carhart as a greedy landowner who doesn't care about his own community, and highlight the value older businesses bring to the village. You can't legally stop him selling, but you could make life difficult for him."

Mary broke into a wide smile.

"You'm more like your grandmother than I realised. I've heard she were a fiery little soul and always getting Mother into trouble with her wild ideas – not that she took much encouraging, I'm sure."

The brief moment of lightness faded and her face settled back into unhappy lines.

"You mean well, my dear, but there's something else…" Mary's chin lifted a touch. "Pat Carhart's offering a bonus to anyone who agrees to give up their lease before the end of the month. If I were ten years older and Mother wasn't around I'd be tempted. I wouldn't be surprised if some of the others take it."

"How much is he offering?" Dan's measured voice sent a shiver down Christa's spine.

"A hundred thousand pounds."

Christa whistled.

"He must be desperate for it to go through quickly."

"So by laying out about six hundred

thousand I'm guessing he'll make around five million." Dan shoved the chair back. "I'm off for a walk to clear my head."

He stormed out of the room and slammed the door behind him. Mary touched Christa's hand as she moved to go after him.

"Leave him be, my love. Dan's always been a fixer. He had to when he was little because my sister was too young to be a good mother, see. Brought himself up really, because his dad wasn't around much. He's mad because he can't see a way to sort this and it makes him feel less of a man."

"It's not his fault. You can't let him blame…"

"He needs to get it out of his system. The problem is you're like him. You want to fix things, too – especially him, don't you?"

Christa couldn't quite meet Mary's piercing eyes.

"If you happened to come across him when you were out doing a bit of shopping for me that'd be a coincidence, wouldn't it?" Mary's eyes shone with mischief.

"I can't wander aimlessly around the village."

"He's always been overly fond of the North Beach. Go down to the harbour and follow the road around to the right. There's a fish shop on the way so you could pick up four nice pieces of cod for our dinner."

Christa jumped up.

"If he asks, I never suggested any of this." Mary wagged a finger at her.

"Don't worry. I'll happily take the blame, and thank you." Christa grinned and ran from the room. She'd track Dan down even if he didn't want her to.

Too Much, Too Soon

CHRISTA picked her way along the rocky beach carrying a bag of fish and struggling to concoct a good excuse for being there. She glanced towards a large outcrop of rocks. Silhouetted in the fading light she spotted Dan and as she approached he awkwardly pulled himself up to standing.

He held out his hand and she jumped up to join him.

"You never give up, do you? I suppose you sweet-talked Aunt Mary into conspiring to find me."

She didn't bother to defend herself.

"You're cold again, aren't you? Don't you ever wear any real clothes?" Dan wrapped his arms around her waist and pressed her up against his warmth.

"Maybe I did it on purpose so you'd have to hug me," she teased.

"You could've asked. You didn't have to

risk hypothermia," he murmured.

"Yeah, but I like to live dangerously."

"I'd noticed." He shifted his weight to the other leg. "Sit with me."

Christa settled down next to him.

"You want to know why I'm in Cornwall."

"Go on, entertain me with your life story to take my mind off all the other stuff," he said with a wry smile.

"You're not getting all the details, partly because we'd freeze to death… The short version is I had a perfectly normal childhood with happily married parents and four older brothers who tormented me. I loathed high school but loved college.

"My first job was at a local newspaper and then I moved to a larger one in Los Angeles. I covered hard news until I tried to expose a corrupt mayor whose family were major shareholders in the paper and I got shifted to covering weddings and boring social events."

She bit her tongue to stop from crying. Christa wondered when she'd stop being angry and only hoped it'd be soon.

Christa hesitated.

"I lost my job because of an argument over a job I didn't want to do." She met Dan's penetrating stare but bit down on the confession she'd almost made. "End of story really. I decided to take a break before starting to job-hunt and I'd wanted to come here for years… so here I am."

"So here you are." He sighed and leaned closer to press a soft kiss on her cheek.

Christa relaxed into his embrace and for a few wonderful seconds nothing else mattered. Then, out of the blue, a picture of Antony telling her how much he loved her filled her head and all she could think was what a bad choice she'd made where he was concerned. She mustn't start anything with Dan beyond friendship, and even that might not be wise. This was all too soon.

She pulled away and slid down over the rock and back on to the beach.

"Hey, where are you going?"

"Sorry, Dan. It's not your fault. It's me. I can't explain right now, maybe some other time." Christa waved the bag of fish and forced a smile. "I need to get this back to Mary."

"Fair enough. I'll be along later." Dan turned away to gaze out over the gleaming black sea.

Christa trailed across the beach and stopped halfway over to glance back over her shoulder but he still faced out towards the horizon. Had she expected him to chase after her? Now she was being ridiculous. The idea to check up on him in the first place was foolish and juvenile, and now she had to face Mary who'd expect a believable explanation for her solo return.

****

Dan strolled into the kitchen, ignored his aunt's curious stare, and switched on the kettle.

"Christa came in a while ago and said jet lag had caught up with her. She went upstairs saying she needed an early night. She didn't look tired to me." She gave her nephew a shrewd look. "Sit down here and put me out of my misery."

Dan sipped his tea.

"Christa was thoughtful enough to come and look for me," he told Mary. "We talked for a while and then she was ready to come back. I stayed a while longer. That's it."

Mary wasn't easily fooled and changing the subject was his only hope.

"Do you want me to take Carhart's letter to the solicitor tomorrow?"

"I suppose it wouldn't hurt." Mary gave him a sly smile. "You could take Christa with you and let her see Truro."

"Maybe. I'm off upstairs to read a while."

Up on the bed he lay on top of the covers, unable to concentrate on his book. Christa Reynolds was an interesting woman, beautiful in her own quirky way and with a smile that could melt gold. She had secrets, too, painful ones and he wanted more than anything to find out who'd hurt her so badly she'd flown from him tonight as if she was being chased by a pack of wild animals.

Sleep wouldn't come tonight so he'd use the time to think instead.

****

Christa threw her heaviest coat on the back seat of Dan's car and climbed into the passenger seat.

"I'd have thought you were the jeep-driving, off-road, gear-crashing type," she joked. "What's with the tame automatic transmission Volvo? Don't most people here drive manual cars?"

Dan's face set into hard lines.

"Yes, but then they don't have one leg that's basically useless as far as strength and movement for driving is concerned."

She cringed at her thoughtlessness, and didn't speak for the rest of the drive.

Dan parked in one of the last available spaces in the small car park and eased out of the car.

"I'm off to see Aunt Mary's solicitor." He pointed across the street to the tall building towering over the small city. "That's the cathedral and the shops are all in the streets around it. Be back here at twelve and we'll eat lunch before returning to Tremorva." He picked up his jacket from the back seat and shrugged it on.

The well-cut dark grey suit, white shirt and forest green tie highlighted his classic good looks and Christa's heart raced. She tried to force herself to be sensible.

Right on time Christa came into sight happily swinging shopping bags in each hand. Dan wished he could brush off his problems as easily. For a few minutes on the beach yesterday he'd wondered if things could be different, but then she'd closed down and he'd come to his senses.

"Hi, again. Truro's so neat and the cathedral's awesome, thanks for bringing me." Christa eyed Dan up and down and grinned. "Abandoned the jacket and tie already? And there was me looking forward to being taken out for lunch by a well-dressed man. You do disappoint a girl."

How was he supposed to resist her sparkling blue eyes and megawatt smile? Even the news he'd got from the solicitor couldn't dull the spark of pleasure she'd ignited inside him.

"I'll make up for it by taking you to the best restaurant this side of London. All locally grown produce, seafood so fresh it was swimming around this morning and a view worthy of being on a postcard."

"Oh, yeah, and I suppose they keep a table free in case you decide to drop in?" she joked.

"Let's just say it's not a problem." Dan tapped the side of his nose.

At the end of a long gravel driveway they pulled to a stop in front of a large old house built of mellow Cornish granite. A large elegantly painted sign proclaimed "Mordros Bay Hotel & Restaurant".

"The name means 'sound of the surf' in Cornish. Appropriate, isn't it?" Dan pointed towards the rugged cliff overlooking the rough crashing ocean a short distance away. He ushered Christa towards the door and it was immediately opened for them.

The hostess didn't get a chance to speak before a loud voice boomed out across the entrance hall.

"Wilson, you old devil. Haven't you got anything better to do on a Monday lunchtime than pester me?"

Plainly this was Dan's secret to getting a table. A handsome ebony-haired man with the same stance as Dan, and a matching regulation haircut headed towards them.

"Not really." Dan slapped the man around the shoulders. "Do something useful and find this beautiful young lady and me a table, and it'd better be one with a good view or you're in trouble."

"So, do I get an introduction?" His low, drawl held the same educated tone as Dan, but was tinged with what she guessed was a hint of Italian heritage.

"Christa. This caveman is Vince D'Amato, owner and manager of this place. We go back a long way." She guessed boarding school and the military. "This is Christa Reynolds. She's American and is visiting for a while. Her grandmother was evacuated to live with my family during the war."

Dan rested a hand on Christa's shoulder in a gesture of possession she rather enjoyed.

"My pleasure, I'm sure." Vince smiled. "I hope you enjoy Cornwall."

A pretty young waitress led them to a round table right by a huge bay window drenched in today's thin, watery sun. Lush tropical plants in oversized ornate planters, white wrought-iron furniture with deep, comfortable yellow cushions, crisp linen tablecloths and stunning black and white china – nothing was as she'd expected.

Their appetiser of grilled sea scallops arrived and she turned her attention to the food. They'd agreed to share a half bottle of wine and the fragrant chardonnay Dan chose was a perfect complement.

"You don't like it much?" Dan laughed as Christa practically inhaled the food and she instantly responded to his happiness.

"How did things go with the attorney?"

"Goodness me, Christa, that sounds so 'LA Law'. Paul Westlake with his tweed jacket and thinning hair isn't that glamorous, trust me." Dan gave a smile.

"I'm guessing he didn't find some obscure clause that'll save the shop or you'd have been bursting to tell me and want to get straight back to Tremorva," she said softly.

He flinched and Christa stretched out her hand and gave his a slight squeeze.

"I'd give anything to return with good news, although I know they're not expecting miracles…"

"They don't happen often." She kept her voice light, far too aware of Dan's fingers stroking her skin.

"Trout for you, sir, and the grilled turbot with hollandaise sauce for the lady."

They stared blankly at the waiter and Dan carefully placed her hand on the table after giving Christa the merest hint of a wink.

She could almost see his mind working, planning his next move, and she wondered what it would be.

****

"If you don't mind braving the wind we could take a walk through the garden?"

Dan didn't want to reveal too much. The element of surprise was a prime military tactic.

Dan took her hand in his, enjoying how small and warm it felt inside his own. He led her along the gravel pathway towards the exposed cliff and at the last moment he steered them into a secluded arbour.

Sheltered from the brisk wind it was fragrant with hundreds of sweet-smelling daffodils in every shade from creamy white to bright sunshine yellow. The sight took his own breath away and he smiled, watching her reaction.

Christa burst into loud, unrestrained laughter.

"You're a sly one, Dan Wilson. You're cleverer than I thought."

He couldn't help smiling again and pulled her down with him on to the white-painted bench. Against all notion of sense he couldn't resist pressing a soft kiss on to her teasing mouth. She sighed and pulled away, regret pooling in her eyes.

"This isn't a good idea."

"Why not?"

"I've recently got out of a serious relationship which proved I'm a bad judge of character, and I'm guessing you've got a lot to sort out in your life before you're up for any kind of commitment."

He frowned.

"You're going way too fast here, slow down. I enjoy your company and I get the impression the feeling's reciprocated. How about we get to know each other a little better and see where it leads us?"

"I'm sorry, I didn't mean to be pushy, but…"

Dan couldn't help grinning.

"Your normal self, you mean?"

"That's me. Like it or not." She smacked his arm.

"I'm beginning to like it pretty well." Dan checked his watch and sighed. "We'd better go. They'll wonder where we are." An insistent pulsing sound interrupted and Dan shoved a hand in his trouser pocket to retrieve his phone. He listened carefully and his expression changed.

He turned back to face Christa.

"That was Gran. Aunt Mary's had an accident at the café and they've taken her to the hospital in Truro. I said we'd go straight there."

"What's happened?" Christa asked.

"She didn't know any details." Dan struggled to hurry towards the car.

"Does your gran need us to pick her up?"

"One of the neighbours took her." Dan gasped and leaned against the car. "Have you still got your bottle of water?"

Christa reached in her bag.

"Are you thirsty?"

Dan managed to open the door and collapsed into the driver's seat. He fumbled in his jacket pocket.

"I need a pain pill." Taking the bottle from her he placed a tablet on his tongue and took a deep swallow of water. It'd take at least twenty minutes to take the edge off the agonising pain in his knee.

She didn't say a word, only took hold of his left hand and Dan closed his eyes, letting the pain wash over him until it eased back to the dull ache he'd learned to live with.

"All right now?" Her quiet concern startled him. "Are you OK to drive?"

"I am now." Dan gave her a swift kiss on the forehead. "Thanks." He didn't dare say any more.

****

Christa held back in the doorway of the waiting room while Dan walked across to hug his grandmother.

"Come over here, love, I could do with seeing your pretty face." Irene beckoned her to join them. "You know what Bea would do if she was here now?" Her eyes sparkled. "She'd get in to see Mary, no matter that we'd been told to stay here."

Dan caught the matching gleam of mischief in Christa's eyes. She sat down, and put on a demure expression which didn't fool him for an instant.

"Gran, why don't you tell Christa some more stories about her grandmother?" They chatted and Dan half-dozed in the uncomfortable plastic chair.

A doctor came in.

"Are you the Treneague family? I'm Doctor Andrew Mawes. Miss Treneague is doing well. She was alert enough to tell me off for using her first name."

Dan calmed down. If his aunt was strong enough to put this young doctor in his place she wasn't in any imminent danger.

"What exactly is wrong? We haven't been told much."

"Miss Treneague got a little careless with a sharp knife and cut a deep gash in her left hand and then fell and hit her head on the floor. The MRI looks good but we want to keep her overnight for observation. We'll be waking her frequently throughout the night to check how she's doing."

Dan smiled. He wouldn't like to be the nurse who got the sharp end of his aunt's tongue at midnight.

"She also strained her back so she'll need to take it easy," the doctor added.

"Can we see her?" Dan asked.

"Only for a few minutes."

"Thanks." He turned to his grandmother. "Let's go and say hello and then we'll go home."

"I don't like leaving her," she protested.

"I'll bring you back first thing in the morning."

Irene touched his cheek.

"You'm a good boy. Come on."

"Why don't you two go and see her on your own?" Christa interrupted. "She doesn't need too many people around."

"Don't be silly, my dear."

"You heard Gran," Dan joined in. "We'll only stay five minutes." He led the way and the second Mary spotted them she glared.

"This nuisance of a man is making me stay the night." Mary glowered at the doctor.

"Quite right, too. Do what you're told for once so we can get you back home tomorrow."

"But what about the café?" Two burning spots lit up Mary's cheeks.

"Don't worry. We'll manage." Dan tried to reassure her.

"You can't. This is the end." Her voice quavered and Christa jumped in.

"No, it's not. We're perfectly capable of running a teashop between us until you're fit again. One of your friends can take care of you at home while Granny Irene comes to the shop. She can give Dan and me instructions and we'll carry them out. End of story."

Mary sank back against the pillow.

"I suppose it might work." Her eyelids drooped, heavy with the effect of the drugs she'd been given. She barely realised when they left.

"So you think you're getting me back in the shop, do you?" Out in the hall, Irene tried to sound stern but her shining eyes betrayed her excitement.

"You must be mad." Dan interjected. "How are an old woman, a crippled man, and a girl who doesn't know one end of a teapot from the other going to run a café? We'll get Julie, the part-time girl, to come and take over. It makes much more sense."

Irene scowled at him.

"Who're you calling useless?"

He tried to protest he hadn't said any such thing but she ploughed right on.

"I can't run around, but there's nothing wrong with my brain or my mouth – I can tell you what to do perfectly well. You're nowhere near as helpless as you make yourself out to be either, and this girl's smart – she'll learn quickly.

Dan threw up his hands in surrender.

"Fine, you're all mad is all I know." He stalked off before they could reply.

Dan's Heartbreak

WITH her hands plunged into a sink full of hot soapy water and sweat-soaked hair stuck to her head, Christa was having second thoughts.

Thank goodness it was only late March so Tremorva was light on tourists. Another week of this and their Gang of Three wouldn't be speaking to each other. They'd unleashed a monster in Irene. From the minute they'd stepped foot in the café at eight yesterday morning she'd turned into a dictator. She'd taken up residence by the cash register and waited to pounce on them for the slightest mistake.

Christa sneaked a glimpse at Dan, grim-faced and determined, standing at the counter making sandwiches. He'd taken his pain medicine halfway through the morning but she'd purposely not commented.

"Christa, dear, we need those dishes when you're done." Irene gazed around her former empire with an air of contentment.

"I'll be finished in a few minutes."

Irene turned her attention to Dan.

"Sit down while it's quiet, dear boy.

"I'm OK. Shall I get us a cup of tea?"

"That'd be nice. I…" Her lip trembled and Christa expected the older woman to burst into tears.

"What's wrong, Gran? We're managing fine."

"It's not that, my love. You just looked so much like your mother for a minute it made me feel strange."

An odd expression crossed Dan's face.

"Oh. Right." He turned away and Christa carried on with her tasks.

Five minutes later Christa combed her hair and put on a slick of bright pink lipstick before bringing through a tray of clean cups and saucers.

"Got time for a breather, have we?"

"If you two can manage for a while I'll take my tea out back and put my feet up." Irene suggested.

Christa took her cup in one hand and helped Irene with the other. With her settled she returned to the empty café.

"So what was all that about? You might as well tell me. I'll get it out of you one way or another." She planted herself right in front of Dan and crossed her arms.

He reached over and ruffled her wild hair, giving a sad smile.

"Yes, I know that. I can't decide if I like that about you, or want to run a mile in the opposite direction." He slapped his injured leg. "Of course, you'd easily catch me, so I suppose I'll stay here and take it."

Christa had never heard him joke about his injury before.

"Out with it then."

"Gran surprised me by saying how much I resembled my mother. That may not sound very unusual to you, but we never talk about her."

"And do you look like her?"

Dan shrugged.

"Maybe."

"Just tell me as much as you want."

"I told you she left here at sixteen for London. She worked at various jobs then met my dad and they married. She was young and didn't know how to be a good mother."

He fell silent and Christa pulled up a stool, took his hands in hers, and said nothing.

"Sometimes the two of us would come here and I always felt safe here with Gran and Aunt Mary."

Christa's heart broke for Dan but knew he'd hate her sympathy and stayed silent.

"My dad was around but he worked long hours and didn't have much time left over for me. When I was eight everything changed." He swallowed hard and she watched his jaw tighten.

"My mother got the flu, she wasn't all that strong and it turned to pneumonia. She passed away and it was just Dad and me. He saved me." Dan's voice cracked and his head dropped into his hands.

"When did he die?" Christa murmured and Dan jerked upright.

"He's not dead, but I've acted like he is since this." He waved in the direction of his leg. "He put me through the best schools and university and I've repaid him by cutting him out of my life. I've not been a good person recently, Christa."

"Do you think I've always been so wonderful?"

He managed a half-smile.

"Oh, I don't know. I've a suspicion you might."

"When did you last see your father?" Dan frowned.

"Just before I came down here a year ago. I'd been in rehab and he'd visited all the time, always with good ideas like taking a job in his business or returning to university for a law degree. I behaved badly and I see it now, but at the time..." He shrugged helplessly.

"Apologise."

"It's not that simple."

About to say "Of course it is", she stopped. Maybe Dan felt his pride was all he had left. She knew it was how she saw life after Antony's bombshell.

"Think about it."

His eyes darkened.

"You don't know how much I do." Dan pulled her into his arms and held her against his warm chest.

"Any chance of a cup of tea when you two have finished? Fine way to run a business, I must say."

Christa stared at the short, stocky businessman in his navy pinstripe suit, pink shirt, and garish purple striped tie.

"Mr Carhart. It's always a pleasure to see you. What can we do for you today?" Dan's voice was cool.

Pat Carhart thrust a bunch of papers in Dan's direction.

"Get your aunt to sign these. I'll have the place in the end so what's the point?"

Dan stood very erect.

"The point is, it's legally ours for the next five months and then we'll see, won't we? Look out of the window."

Carhart glanced out on the harbour then back to Dan.

"At what?"

"Do you see hell freezing over?" Dan carried straight on, "No? That's right and you won't because you'll get this place over my dead body."

"You haven't heard the last of this." Carhart stormed from the café, slamming the door behind him.

Irene appeared in the kitchen doorway.

"What was all the noise about?"

"Pat Carhart was here. We exchanged a few words and he left rather abruptly," Dan told her.

Irene laughed.

"I expect he deserved it. He were a nasty piece of work as a child and never got any better." She laughed at Christa's surprise. "You thought I'd tell Dan off, didn't you? There's probably no chance of saving the café, but that doesn't mean we've got to like it and be pleasant to him."

Turning back to the counter Dan started to wrap paper napkins around cutlery for the tables.

"By the way, Gran, I told Christa about my mother."

"Good." Irene clutched her hands together. "Dan, my love, you've only to say if you want to talk about Lizzie. We always thought it were best not to, but maybe we were wrong."

He didn't answer but he gripped the pile of forks so tightly Christa was surprised they didn't break.

"Some of us have work to do. What do you want done next, Granny Irene?"

Christa tried to take the older woman's attention away from Dan.

"Don't ask me to make pasties, though. I studied Julie earlier and thanked my lucky stars we'd got her in to help."

Irene's smile returned.

"Don't worry, my dear. We'd like to stay open until Mary returns and, no offence, if you made the pasties we'd be closed in a matter of days."

Christa laughed and tossed her head in mock disdain.

"I'm off to the kitchen."

"Best place for a woman." Dan teased and she stuck her tongue out before flouncing off.

* * * *

"I'm off to get Aunt Mary." Dan checked the time. "Will you two be all right here until I get back?"

"I expect we'll survive, young man. Make sure Mrs Rowe is there before you leave your aunt at home." Irene wagged a finger at him.

"Would you like me to come and fetch you after they're settled? The afternoon tea crowd will be pretty much done by then and we could finish up, couldn't we, Christa?"

She blushed under the power of his smile.
"Yeah, no problem."

"If you're sure, I'd be some pleased to see
how she's doing."

Dan grabbed his cane and limped out of
the door.

Irene instantly turned to Christa with a
frown.

"You won't hurt my boy, will you?"

"One of the reasons I left Los Angeles
was to get away from... some bumps in my
private life. Don't worry, I'm not looking for
anything more than friendship."

"I'm sorry, love." She patted Christa's
hand. "It's only that Dan's precious to me."

"I know, and I care for him, too." She
risked a grin. "I don't mind admitting I think
he's cute, though."

"He's a handsome one with a kind heart.
A girl could do worse."

Christa laughed.

"I have done – many times."

****

A light drizzle settled on the windows and
Christa's mind drifted to Monterey and her
family. She ought to call home tonight but
her mom would have a fit to hear she
wasn't thinking of leaving any time soon. If
Christa admitted to baking scones and

cakes she'd roar with laughter. Antony had
always mocked her lack of domestic talents,
too, but not in a kind way.

Christa wiped at her cheek, surprised to
discover tears tracking down her skin. She
glanced at her left hand and rubbed the
place where her engagement ring was for
eight long months. All those plans and for
what? So he could go off and marry
another woman and leave her adrift.

Was this how Dan felt? All his life plans fell
apart and he couldn't see what to replace
them with. Suddenly she understood him.

"Hey, are you OK?"

She spun round to find staring Dan oddly
at her.

"Why wouldn't I be?"

"Uh, because you've been crying."

Christa bristled.

"I think that's my own business."

"You don't have to tell me anything, but
it might do some good." He tenderly
stroked her jaw, forcing her to meet his
eyes. "You helped me earlier, you know."

"Oh, Dan. I can't today but I will soon.
Promise."

He pressed a light kiss on her mouth.

"All right, but I'm here if you change your
mind."

"Thanks."

"No problem. I think we'd better start

clearing up."

"How about I do a very American thing
and demand a rain check on talking more?"

"We can't go out anywhere until Aunt
Mary's better, but how about a date in the
garden tonight?" Dan slid his hands down
to circle her waist. "Is ten o'clock too late?"

"Perfect."

"Right, for now it's more dishes to wash."
He laughed and she grinned back before
giving him a teasing smack on the arm.

"Slave driver."

Confession Time

MARY stretched out on the sofa, propped
up with a selection of cushions. With her
appetite plainly unaffected by the accident
she'd managed several ham sandwiches
plus a slice of fruit cake and was now
working on a jam and cream scone.

Christa kneeled on the floor and toyed
with a slice of chocolate cake.

"Eat up, love." Mary scolded. "You'm
nothing but skin and bone. Your mother
will think I haven't been feeding you."

Mary switched her attention to Dan.

"Mother told me you had a barney with
Pat Carhart today."

"I suppose this pair came home telling

tales?" He gestured towards Christa and his grandmother.

"Dan, I'm not cross, my love." Mary looked abashed. "I turn into a jelly around the man." Her eyes filled with tears.

Dan came over to hug his aunt.

"It was only hot air because what can I do? I don't have the money to buy him out and that's the only way we're going to beat him," he said ruefully.

Mary rested a hand on his arm.

"I've been thinking about what Christa said and wonder if it's worth a try."

"You mean about mounting a publicity campaign?" Christa couldn't suppress her excitement. "If you want my help, I'm in. I haven't any experience about doing that sort of thing here but it can't be that different. I don't suppose you did any kind of PR work in the Marines, Dan?"

He gave a twisted smile.

"No. My work didn't involve newspaper articles and peaceful protests."

Everyone went quiet but Christa went on.

"Fine. I'd suggest a meeting of all the shop owners first. Can you organise that, Aunt Mary? I'll put together a rough agenda and we'll go from there." She caught Dan's admiring glance and the colour rose in her cheeks.

"I'll ring everyone this evening when

they've closed up and see if they can come tomorrow." Mary beckoned Christa closer and planted a big kiss on her cheek. "Your granny would be right proud of you."

Christa blushed again.

"Well, we haven't done anything yet."

"Yes, we have. We're not giving in so easily and that's made me feel better than anything. I only wish I were up and about. I'm not made for lying around." She waved in disgust at her bandaged hand.

Dan started to pick up the tea things.

"I understand, but you haven't got any choice. If you do what you're told you'll be up and about again faster. That's what I heard for nearly six months so you can hack it for a few days. Teaches you patience if nothing else."

Christa burst out laughing.

"Really? Didn't do a very good job with you, did they?"

"Like you'd know what patience is – is the word in the American dictionary?" He scoffed.

"All right, children." Mary chipped in. "For your punishment you can wash up the tea dishes and I don't care if you have been washing dishes all day."

"Why don't people here have dishwashers?" Christa sighed.

"They do – they're called hands." Dan

grabbed hers and planted a kiss on each yellow rubber-gloved finger.

She splashed soapy water at him, dabbing some on the end of his nose.

"Behave. I'll wash and you wipe." Christa flicked the dish towel hard enough to sting his arm and laughed as he jumped back.

"Women." Dan pulled up a tall stool and perched on it.

Christa got busy and hummed as she worked away. She'd never been very domestic before but doing chores seemed different here. The first batch of scones she made were so good she'd been proud of herself. For a foreigner she wasn't doing too badly.

"Hey. Are you coming back from dreamland any time soon?"

"Did you say something?" She turned to Dan, guessing he'd spoken to her.

"I asked if you were going to come back from wherever it was you'd drifted away to?" His finger lifted her chin to meet his curiosity.

Christa gazed into his warm brown eyes, reminding her of glossy melted Hershey chocolate. She glanced down at the sink.

"Two more cups and we're done. What's on the agenda for the evening?"

Dan finished drying and hung up the towel. He gave a lazy grin and slid his arms around her waist.

"I've never seen a lady look so adorable over a sink of dirty dishes."

"Aren't you full of compliments tonight?" She kept it light, wondering how Antony's image seemed to be fading around this interesting man.

"I've hear it said the Brits have no imagination but I try my best." Dan's smile warmed her heart. "Remember to be in the garden at ten."

"What happens if I'm not?"

His mischievous laughter filled the room. "I wouldn't want to find out."

****

Cornwall turned on a warm moonlit night especially for them. At least that's how it struck Christa. She came out to the garden early to savour the anticipation of his arrival.

"Hey, beautiful." Dan appeared out of nowhere and slid on the bench next to her.

He pulled her into a gentle embrace.

She couldn't put it off any longer, no matter how easy it'd be to give in to merely enjoying his company. The time had come to tell him...

"I need to tell you about Antony," she insisted.

"Now?"

"I'm sorry." Christa pulled gently away.

"That's OK. Go ahead."

She sucked in a deep breath for courage.

"I was too shy to date in high school, and college wasn't much better. After graduation I was a typical LA single girl with a busy social life, but no steady boyfriend. Then I met Antony." She hesitated and embarrassment warmed her face.

"I was twenty-five and he was ten years older and my boss. Clichéd, isn't it?"

"Did you date him for a while?"

"Yeah, nearly five years. My folks never did like Antony."

"Often our families see what we don't or can't for ourselves." Dan declared with a tired smile.

"On New Year's Eve last year I gave him an ultimatum and he proposed. I was turning thirty and I guess I panicked, which was silly."

Dan stroked her cheek and she leaned into his touch.

"I must be a failure, too, seeing I'm thirty-five and never been engaged or married."

"Have you ever come close?"

"No," he hesitated.

Christa continued.

"You know what a steamroller weddings are. It was easy to talk to Antony about mundane things like flower colours and the choice of chicken or salmon for the reception."

"That would rivet me, I must say."

She loved his dry humour and cracked a smile right back.

"I refused to see things weren't right, but a week before the wedding Antony told me he couldn't go through with it." Tears ran down her cheeks as she remembered how awful she'd felt, as if her world had ended.

Dan pulled her into his arms and gently stroked her cropped hair.

"I'm sorry, my sweet."

"After we split it was tough. Through the work grapevine I heard Antony was dating a young intern, but it was still a shock when their wedding announcement came in. I told my editor I couldn't write the story and lost my job." She eked out a smile. "That's my sad tale. I don't have much to offer you right now."

"Isn't that up to me to decide?"

"I'm only here for a short visit so how about we stick to our original plan and enjoy each other's company without worrying about next week or next month?"

"Sounds good to me."

"You are such a martyr." Christa managed a genuine laugh this time.

"That's me. Dan the hero at your service."

She held his gaze in hers and her heart

did a somersault, pretty sure this man had
her hooked – and not at all sure she wanted
to wiggle off the line.

****

"Did you sleep well, Christa? It's tiring
standing all day when you're not used to
it." Aunt Mary asked, a teasing smile
lighting up her eyes.

"Uh, not too badly, thanks. The time
change is still bothering me some so it's
hard to get off to sleep." Christa mashed
the cornflakes further down into the milk.

Irene joined in.

"I'm a typical old woman these days –
sleep all evening in the chair and stay
awake half the night. There was a nice bit
of moonlight last night so I could look out
over the garden to the sea when I was up
wandering around."

Dan should've guessed nothing would go
unnoticed with his nosey relatives around,
even an innocent chat in the garden.

"I'll clear the dishes. It's time we made a
move to open up." Christa stood up, her
face flushed with embarrassment.

"I'll help." Dan grabbed the tray and
carelessly piled things on in his haste to
avoid any further inquisition.

As they reached the kitchen the sound of

62

laughter drifted down the hallway. Dan
banged the tray down on the table.

"Can no-one have a private life around
here?" he grouched.

"Oh, don't be an old stick-in-the-mud."
She laughed. "They're no different than my
terrible brothers who've teased me since
the day I was born."

"I don't mean to be unkind." Dan
touched her arm. "Our friendship is special
to me and I don't want anyone spoiling it."

"It's special to me, too."

He couldn't put into words how she made
him feel, didn't understand it himself yet.
Dan dropped a quick kiss on her cheek.

"Come on, time to get busy. You wash –
I'll wipe – then we'll go and do it all over
again for the whole day. Fun, isn't it? Are
you glad you came?"

Christa's simple nod made him absurdly
pleased.

They finished and got ready to go, almost
making it to the front door before his aunt
caught up with them.

"Make sure you get back quickly tonight.
We'll have us a little bit of tea before
everyone comes at six." Mary admonished
them.

Dan promised and almost dragged Christa
out the front door.

After nearly ten hours and a steady

stream of customers they were finally done. Dan parked outside the house and for a few seconds they sat in the car. Christa rested her head on his shoulder as he threaded his fingers through her hair and massaged the tension from her scalp.

"What a long day. I'd love a hot bath and supper in bed." She sighed.

"Me, too, but we need to get inside before Mary sends out a search party. You know she'll have heard the car arrive."

"All right, boss." Christa got out and headed inside the house, wondering how the evening ahead of them would go.

All too soon everyone arrived and was set up with cups of tea and slices of Mary's delicious chocolate cake. There was no excuse to put off starting any longer but Christa was strangely nervous. For a start they'd surely have trouble understanding her accent; she'd had a few problems in the café already.

This wasn't really any of her business and maybe she shouldn't be interfering. She became aware of Dan's attention fixed on her, warming her with his smiling eyes and giving her a burst of confidence.

"Hi, everyone. Mary's asked me to say a few words and I daren't refuse or I'll be put on starvation rations tomorrow." Everyone laughed and Christa's apprehension eased.

"When she told me about the problem with your businesses I came up with a few suggestions and she wants me to share them with you. Legally there's nothing we can do to stop Mr Carhart, but if we get out a ton of publicity about your cause and stir up public opinion we can make his life very difficult.

"Why don't you all tell me who you are, which shop is yours and whether you're inclined to accept Mr Carhart's early buyout offer."

People exchanged uncomfortable glances and Christa mentally kicked herself. When would she learn how much more tactfully things needed to be done here?

"If you don't want to commit yet that's fine, ignore it for now."

Still nobody spoke.

"I'll go first if you're all going to sit around like a bunch of lemons." A stunning young woman with flashing green eyes and waist length black hair jumped up from the sofa. Her colourful trailing garments floated with the sudden movement and the assortment of bracelets around her wrists jangled.

"I'm Jenna Branch and I run the Krystal Kabin. This place is my destiny so I'm definitely not taking the money. He'll have to drag me out of there," she declared.

Before Christa could reply a grey-haired older man interrupted.

"Be careful who you call a lemon, young lady. You haven't been in the village five minutes and my family's lived in Tremorva for ten generations." He turned towards Christa. "John Penmount at your service, Miss Reynolds. I own 'Books by the Yard' which of course is a self-explanatory name."

"Get on with it, you pompous old fool. Are you in or out?"

Christa stared at the tall young man sprawled on the carpet, looking like a refugee from a Californian beach with his shoulder-length blond hair, garish board shorts, tanned skin and tattoos.

"We haven't got all day. It's stupid to waste time…"

"Robbie Wilks, I'll wash your mouth out with soap if you don't mind your language," Irene snapped.

He flung himself at her feet in a dramatic apology and soon she laughed and called him a naughty boy. Sitting back on his square of floor he flashed a mischievous smile at Christa.

"Robbie Wilks, at your service." He bowed like a latter day Robin Hood. "My place of business is 'Surf's Up' if you hadn't guessed. The same as our esteemed book shop owner my family's been here for ever. I escaped for a while, but like a bad penny I returned." He scrutinised her closely. "If you're looking for a job I could do with a real California girl to liven things up."

"She doesn't need a job. Can we stick to the business in hand, please?" Dan rested his arm on Christa's shoulder.

"Hey, sorry." Robbie tossed up his hands.

Christa focused back on Robbie, annoyed and pleased at Dan's proprietary gesture at the same time.

"I assume you're with us?"

"Yes, count me in."

She turned to the other woman in the group who was her own mother's age.

"And you are?"

"Emma Tregorick – Piskies Galore."

Robbie interrupted.

"She sells the junk the tourists love – sticks of rock and cheap models of Cornish piskies on toadstools."

"You're a very rude man." Emma dismissed him and then stared defiantly around the room. "I've already accepted Mr Carhart's offer and plan to move near my sister in Torquay."

"Fair enough. Let's carry on," Christa continued and looked over at a well-dressed man in the corner by Mary.

"Marc Trelawney. Ex-lawyer, incomer from

the dreaded London and now owner of 'Leather Lines'. I'm with you. I came here to get away from people like Carhart. I don't need the money and don't want to see the horrible man damage the character of this village."

His clipped standard English was much easier to understand than the heavy Cornish accents of the others and his restrained support bolstered her confidence.

"Thanks." She hesitated, unsure where to go next.

John Penmount looked around at everyone in turn.

"I'm with the majority. No Penmount man's loyalty has ever been bought, and I don't intend being the first."

"Well said, John," Mary praised him. "I feel exactly the same. Emma, I respect your choice but I'm disappointed in you."

The other woman fiddled with her handbag strap, not quite meeting anyone's eyes before speaking again.

"I'm going now. I wish you all well, but please leave me out of your plans."

As the door closed behind her an uneasy silence settled on the room.

"Where are we going to start?"

Jenna's direct question startled Christa. She'd stuck her nose into their business and now had to follow through.

"I'll draft out petitions for you to have in your shops. You need to stir your customers up against Carhart's scheme. I'll put together a press release and get it in the newspapers. Has anybody got any contacts?"

John Penmount nodded.

"My cousin's an editor at the 'Cornish Times' so that won't be a problem."

"Great. Anyone else?" All Christa received were blank stares. "Right. I'll get the petitions made and bring them to you. That way I can see your shops at the same time to help me with the background story." She wasn't sure what else to say.

In less than ten minutes the four of them were on their own again and Mary nodded over at her mother.

"Just in time to watch 'Coronation Street'. We'll have a sandwich later to make up for not having much tea."

"I expect Christa could do with something more substantial after being on her feet all day." Dan jumped in.

"How about I take her down to the Bosun's Locker for a bite to eat? We'll leave you to watch your show in peace."

****

"There you go, one large white wine. I've ordered scampi and chips for us both, if that's OK?" Dan asked. "Is this better than staying in?" He relaxed back in the chair, took a swallow of his beer and grinned.

"Yeah, much, but you know I'm not hungry, don't you?"

"You will be." He said complacently and of course he was right.

Soon she was trawling through a plate of golden scampi and the best thick-cut French fries she'd ever eaten in her life. He even persuaded her to try malt vinegar instead of ketchup on her fries, only he called them chips – remembering all these different names was hard.

She finished and laid down her knife and fork. Glancing up it was hard to miss the satisfaction on Dan's face.

"Liked that, did you?"

"You did, too," she retorted, pointing at his empty plate.

"I'm getting a Coke. Would you care for more wine?"

Christa shook her head and let him go, wishing she didn't enjoy his company quite as much. She should be sensible and get the conversation back to the publicity campaign. As soon as Dan sat back down she launched into a rambling explanation of her ideas. He let her talk for five minutes before he reached over and picked up her hands.

"Tomorrow you can be efficient and organised and I'll do whatever I can to help, but we're not going to waste the rest of the evening on the best wording for a petition."

The soft kiss he rested on her mouth left her no choice.

"Captain Wilson?"

A young woman suddenly appeared by their table, frowning and fiddling with the ends of her long, dark hair.

Dan gave a brief nod, obviously annoyed at the interruption.

"I'm Sarah Alexander, from Mordros Bay. I'm sorry to bother you, but..." She glanced from Dan to Christa and back again.

"It's OK. Carry on. This is Christa Reynolds and she's well behaved – for an American."

Sarah's pale skin flushed.

"It's Vince – Mr D'Amato, I should say, but he makes us call him Vince. Sorry."

"Sit down, please. I'll get you a drink and you can tell me what's wrong."

"I don't need anything." She plucked at the sleeve of her pale pink sweater. "About an hour ago a woman turned up and started screaming at Vince in front of all the guests. They were speaking in Italian so I'm not sure what was being said, but they were both angry. He asked me to get you."

"My car's in the next street over. You go on back to the hotel and I'll be with you in about half an hour."

"Thanks. We'll see you soon."

Sarah smiled and left.

"Are you ready?" Dan held out his hand.

Christa hadn't liked to assume he'd want her along.

"You didn't think I'd go without you, did you?" Dan pulled her up to join him.

Christa's mother said she might be bored in quiet, unexciting Cornwall. There was absolutely no chance of that.

A Friend In Need…

IS the woman still here?"

"No." Sarah replied. "She left while I was fetching you. That was when Vince stormed off up to his room and now he won't come out or talk to anyone."

Dan shoved his fingers through his hair.

"I'll go up. Send Christa up with a tray of coffee in a few minutes." He limped towards the stairs and made his way slowly to the first floor.

"Open up, mate."

Vince's door cracked open a few inches and Dan quickly stepped inside.

"Go and sit down." He heard Christa coming and poked his head back out to take the tray from her.

It was a long slow hour of difficult conversation before he got away, pleased to find Christa waiting.

"Sorry. Do you mind getting Sarah? Vince fell asleep but I'd be happier if someone was with him and I don't think she'll mind."

"Will he be OK?"

"Yeah. I'll pop over in the morning and talk to him some more. I'll tell you the full story then. Tonight's version was garbled to say the least."

She rested her soft hand on his arm.

"You're a good friend."

"It's nothing to what he's done for me in the past, trust me."

"Let's go." Her sympathy touched him somewhere deep inside where he'd thought it was frozen for ever.

****

"What have you two got planned for today?" Mary asked. "And before you say anything, I'm perfectly capable of taking over again at the café. You can get your coat and come, too, Mum, no more easy days for you."

"I'll be down later to see everyone in their shops, take some photos and ask more questions. That should keep me busy."

"That's good, dear. How about you, Dan?"

"I'm heading over to Mordros Bay to see Vince. He wasn't feeling too good last night. I'm not sure how long I'll be, so don't plan on me being around for lunch."

He limped from the room and Christa decided she'd be wise to get away before Mary interrogated her.

She ran out behind him and he pulled her into a brief hug. Dan eased back and grinned before ruffling her hair.

"The colour's fading and it doesn't prickle my fingers any more. You might resemble a normal woman soon."

She smacked his arm but he only laughed, giving her another heart-stopping smile.

"I'll see you later," Dan whispered.

"I hope Vince is OK."

"Yeah, me, too. This problem might not be easy to solve."

"You'll do your best." Christa smiled and ran off up the stairs – unable to trust herself not to say something foolish.

****

Christa rested up against her bedroom door, her mind racing.

This was getting her nowhere. She brushed her hair and applied some lipstick then gathered up her camera, laptop and notebook. Before she left the room she grabbed a raincoat and umbrella, grinning as she did so – Dan's "be prepared" personality was catching.

The air was heavy with the scent of the sea and Christa lingered down by the harbour and took in the scene around her.

Small delivery vans braved the narrow streets and a window cleaner tackled the never-ending layer of salt off a shop window. One woman talked to a neighbour while leaning on the sweeping brush that was little more than a prop for conversation.

Christa whipped out her camera and took pictures for an article she would try to write one day. A face appeared in front of the lens and she gave a startled yelp.

"Morning, gorgeous." Robbie Wilks gave a lazy smile, obviously pleased to have surprised her.

"You're a menace. Haven't you anything better to do?"

He slid an arm around her shoulder and grinned.

"I do now."

"I came to find out more about your shop and take some photos, nothing else."

"Hey, a man's entitled to try."

Christa burst out laughing.

"You're impossible."

"Come on in and I'll make you some real coffee. You won't get better anywhere here."

She nodded.

"That's a deal."

An hour later she'd been revived by his excellent fresh ground coffee and picked up a load of information. He'd given her the lowdown on all the other owners and shops plus a lot of background on the Carhart family. For a laid-back young man she'd discovered Robbie was a goldmine.

Her next conversation with Jenna at the Krystal Kabin was an exercise in patience. It was hard to get much sense from someone who talked to crystals and wanted to read Christa's aura. She breathed a sigh of relief as she escaped.

Next stop was the bookshop. John Penmount knew a lot but also loved the sound of his own voice. Christa wished she hadn't mentioned his family when he spent a half hour boring her about every generation of Penmounts back to the first sailors who'd ended up in Tremorva.

She hadn't intended to go into Piskies Galore, but was lured by the cute figurines littering the window display. A cute amber-eyed one posed on a rock sparked off happy recollections of Dan.

"Miss Reynolds, I'm shocked at you for stepping foot on enemy territory."

Emma Tregorick's friendly smile made Christa uncomfortable.

"I'm not here for any devious purpose. There's something in the window I'm interested in."

"I can't turn down a sale, so what can I help you with?"

After they got the purchase sorted Christa wandered around the the shop. On her way out she couldn't resist one last attempt.

"Won't you miss this place? You must have lived here a long time?" A shaft of pain crossed Emma's face and Christa wished she'd kept her mouth shut.

"Yes, I will. I've been in the village all my fifty-five years. I have my reasons." She turned away and fiddled with the price labels on some books.

"Sorry." She must be losing her journalistic thick skin because Christa honestly did regret asking.

There was still Leather Lines and the café to go, but Christa was worn out and more than ready for lunch. She didn't dare hope Dan would walk around the corner...

Christa turned her phone back on to see one message. "Meet me at the Bosun's Locker at one." The man must be a mind reader. "I need your advice." It must be connected with Vince and she loved the prospect of an interesting story. Dan would tell her to mind her own business, but she could easily get around him.

She hummed as she strolled towards the pub. So far today was very satisfying and promised to become even more so.

****

Thankfully, Dan knew the sharp curves and narrow lanes well as he headed back into Tremorva, his mind still mulling over Vince's confession.

His friend had greeted him clutching a mug in his hand.

"Hey, mate, have you come to scrounge free coffee off me again."

"Cheers to you, too. I'll go back home and leave you to it if you want."

"I'm sure Sarah will find an extra cup. If nothing else it'll prise her away from my side for a minute." The touch of pleasure in his voice said he didn't really mind.

Sure enough she fussed around, settling them in a quiet corner of the sun room, and giving Vince a slight pat on the shoulder before leaving them alone.

"Now you can tell me how badly I made a fool of myself last night." Vince smiled ruefully.

"Everyone loses their temper occasionally, no big deal."

"I shouldn't have overreacted that way but... you know I stayed in Italy a while after I was injured in Iraq the first time?" Vince asked.

"Didn't you go with some of your family down around Naples?"

Vince stared at his hands.

"Yeah." He drew in a deep breath. "I met a woman called Bella. We got involved and I think she felt sorry for me." Vince glanced down at the floor and back up at Dan. "We kind of ended up married."

"Married?" He couldn't believe what he was hearing, this was the one person he'd thought he knew inside and out.

"I wanted to tell you at the time but you were having a hard time so I didn't. Bella didn't want to leave her family there and we realised it'd basically been a holiday romance that got out of hand. We parted with no hard feelings and I didn't hear from her again."

"Did she come chasing after you yesterday?" Dan struggled to make sense of the bizarre story.

"No. That was her mother."

"Why now?"

"She had some news and I didn't take it too well. Apparently Bella kept to herself the fact she had our baby. I've got a four-year-old daughter, Dan. Bella died last month and asked her mother to get me to help raise little Isabella. What am I going to do? I can't bring up a child."

Panic ran through his words.

"Look at these." He tossed a pile of photos down on the table and Dan picked one up. A beautiful little laughing black-haired, dark-eyed girl, the absolute image of Vince.

Something about the story puzzled Dan.

"How come the grandmother's willing to hand the child over to a stranger?"

"Because she's got a heart condition and is afraid she won't be around much longer to take care of Isabella. There are no other family members young enough to help out either. We argued because I told her I needed time to think and she's coming back tomorrow. What on earth am I going to tell her?"

"Let me go away and have a think. How about I come back tonight and we'll talk some more?"

Vince nodded.

"Don't blab this around, please, especially not to your little American. She's the nosey type, I can tell."

This wasn't his story to tell but how could he not share with her what was on his mind? Did love usually tangle a man up this way? Love? Caring. Attraction. It couldn't be anything more for now.

Dan pulled into the pub car park with his

knee aching like mad. He washed a pain pill down with some water and waited.

****

Why didn't Dan go on in? Christa waited in the shadow of the butcher's shop until he got out and limped towards the pub, leaning heavily on his cane. Her journalist's mind began to invent myriad reasons Dan might want to talk and none were good.

Maybe it was nothing to do with Vince and that'd been merely a ploy to get her here. Perhaps he wanted to break their relationship and didn't know how.

She took her time and Dan tried to stand as she made her way across the room.

"Don't, please." She urged him to sit back down. "I'll get our drinks. Do you want your usual pint?"

"No, thanks. I'll stick to soda water and lime today. Alcohol and strong pain medicine don't mix." He gave a wry smile.

She nodded and headed over to the bar, successfully getting the barman's attention then wended her way back through the crowd of people. Christa picked up the menu and pretended to study it.

"Do you want to order lunch now or later?"

Part of her wanted to insist on now, but

the food would choke in her throat.

"I guess we can wait." Christa sat back in her chair and met Dan's intense gaze. Today she wished his eyes weren't that tempting shade of chocolate brown.

"Let's get this over with. You've obviously decided our friendship is over. I'm not sure why, but that's your prerogative. I'll stay and help with the shops protest then flit off back to California." The menu slipped from her hands on to the floor but she made no effort to pick it back up.

"What on earth are you talking about?" His quiet voice made her pulse race.

"You said in the message you needed to talk."

He shook his head in disbelief.

"I said I wanted your advice, and from that you made up this crazy story?"

"Oh, Dan. Do you really blame me with my track record?"

"Maybe your ex-fiancé was dumb but I'm not. What I want to talk about has nothing to do with us, I promise."

"Oh." Tears pressed against her eyes and she fought to hold them in.

Dan reached over to take hold of her hands, wrapping them in his warm strength.

"I don't know about you, but I'm starving. Now we've established no-one's trying to dump anybody, why don't we go ahead and eat. My story will wait."

Her stomach rumbled on cue and they both cracked up, drawing curious looks from the other patrons.

"I'll take that as your answer." He pulled some money from his wallet. "Would you mind ordering? Pushing through this crowd when I'm... not too good..."

"Don't apologise, of course I'll go. Do you want scampi and chips again?" She grinned and jumped up. Christa made their order and got back to him as fast as she could.

This time she pulled her chair close and rested her head on his shoulder.

Sam shouted over.

"Scampi and chips. Twice."

"Saved by the fish," Dan quipped and gave Christa a brief kiss as she stood up to get their food.

"Any chance of us taking a drive somewhere quiet?" Christa asked when they'd finished eating.

"Of course." Awkwardly he eased back up to standing and she slipped her arm through his, waiting while he picked up his cane. "I know the ideal spot."

"Why am I not surprised?" She smiled and let Dan led the way.

Out Of The Blue

YOU want to grab that?" Dan pointed to
a red tartan blanket on the back seat. "I
know a good place a short way off the
path." Penwarren Woods was one of his
favorite spots.

Ten minutes of gentle walking and they
entered the small glade surrounded by tall,
dark trees, drenched in sunlight and
cushioned with delicate white flowers and
soft grass.

"Wow, this is seriously gorgeous."

Dan spread out the blanket.

"Let's sit." He eased himself down and
held out his hand for her to join him. She
made herself comfortable and leaned in to
rest her head on his shoulder. The soft,
trusting gesture loosened his tongue.

"I saw Vince this morning and he shared
what happened yesterday. It'll probably be
common knowledge soon, but for now
we've got to keep it to ourselves."

"Vince asked you not to tell me, didn't
he?" Dan flushed with embarrassment and
Christa touched his hand.

"It's OK. He doesn't know me. I don't
blame him. If you don't feel able to share,
that's OK, too."

"But I want to. I need your take on this."
He wondered if she knew what a huge step
this was for him – for them. Dan launched
into the whole story.

"Wow. Not what I expected." Christa
shook her head in disbelief.

"So, what do you think he should do?"

"I'd suggest he visits them in Newquay
instead of having them come to the hotel
only because it'd be more private. Maybe he
could ask the grandmother to stay for a few
weeks while they sort things out. You can't
rip a child from the only family she's known
and drop her in a strange country.
Presumably she doesn't even speak English."

Dan rubbed at his throbbing knee.

"I hadn't thought of that. I don't suppose
so. Vince is scared. I said I'd go back over to
see him tonight."

"The panic will have worn off by now.
You can throw out my suggestions if you
want and say they're yours. And I'll tape my
mouth shut – promise."

He leaned over to give her a soft kiss.

****

After supper Christa gazed out of her
bedroom window and her eyes strayed up
to the rhododendron blocking her view of
the secret seat in the corner. Merely

thinking about Dan made her feel warm inside.

"Christa, Aunt Mary's got some news when you come down." Dan shouted in through the door, his gorgeous voice making her tingle all over.

"I'll be there in a minute. You go on." Christa needed to pull herself together. She worked a dab of gel through her hair, added a quick slick of pink lipstick and she was ready.

"Have a look at this, my dear, you've done a right proper job." Mary thrust the local newspaper at Christa the moment she walked into the room.

She read it through and nodded.

"Not too bad."

"None of us could've done as well and John says the paper's had lots of calls from people wanting to show their support." Mary beamed.

Christa hated to dampen her enthusiasm but was realistic. In the scheme of things this was only the beginning. Pat Carhart wasn't going to give up millions of pounds because of one measly article.

"That's great. Now we have to build on this." She glanced at Dan. "What do you think should be our next move?"

He looked thoughtful for a moment.

"Maybe you could get the local radio

station on board and wangle yourself an interview. After that, try the TV network. The more publicity we can get the more pressure there'll be on Carhart. If you can force him to defend himself he'll come over badly. He's an outspoken man."

"That's perfect."

Dan flushed.

"Good. If you'll all excuse me, I'm off to see Vince."

"Are you going along, too, Christa?" Mary probed.

"No, it's boys' night tonight." Let them think he was going to socialise. She wouldn't be the one to give away Vince's secret.

****

A child's pathetic wails drifted down the stairs. Sarah headed towards the kitchen and raised her eyes to the heavens as she went by. Dan made his way upstairs to Vince's rooms and walked into chaos.

His friend was kneeling in front of the sofa and a little red-faced girl was beating her hands on the cushions, her legs kicking wildly against the furniture. She appeared to have blobs of pasta and sauce all over her yellow dress, some of it stuck in her tangle of black curly hair.

Vince looked at Dan in despair.

"Wilson, come here and meet Issy." The child berated her father in fluent Italian. "I'm sorry. I should have said Isabella Maria D'Amato. The pasta wasn't up to her usual standard and she's not happy because her grandmother left this afternoon." Vince's voice resonated with panic.

"Left? How could she?"

"Easily. She put one foot in front of the other and walked outside to a taxi." Vince waved his arm helplessly around the room. "She left me Isabella, two suitcases of clothes and her passport and birth certificate."

Dan was at a complete loss. Christa's suggestions were a waste of breath now.

"Shouldn't you get her bathed?"

"You try. She kicks and bites anyone who comes near. She won't even let Sarah touch her and there's no sweeter creature living. What about that woman of yours? Has she got any experience with children?"

"I don't know. She'd suggested a..." Dan's voice trailed away and Vince grinned.

"Told her, didn't you?"

Dan stood mute.

"I knew you would. That's OK. Will you call her? Please. See if she's any ideas." Vince sounded desperate.

"I'll have to go and fetch her if she'll

come. She won't drive. Says we're all
lunatics who ought to be forced to drive on
the right side of the road and cringes when
I come within inches of a hedge."

Vince snorted.

"Your driving would scare anyone."

"Watch it, or I'll leave you to solve this
yourself." Dan gave a fake glare and
opened up his mobile phone. He walked
outside the room to speak, not knowing
how much the kid understood. He kept the
conversation brief before going back in.

"I'm off to get Christa."

Would they ever get an uninterrupted
evening together?

****

"So, what's up with Vince?" Mary asked
pointedly and Christa fought to stop the
heated blush rushing towards her cheeks.

"I've no idea what you mean. Dan wants
to take me for a walk, that's all." A firm
stare and an outright lie was the best she
could come up with.

"On the Mordros Bay cliffs, in the dark?
Very sensible."

She exhaled with relief as Dan's car pulled
into the driveway and said her goodbyes
before she could be pinned down any more.

Christa gripped the door handle and

prayed they wouldn't meet another car on the dark narrow roads.

"We're there, you can open your eyes again, coward." Dan flashed a cheeky grin. "Come on, let's go in so you can meet the little monkey." The edges of his smile faded and she guessed his own childhood memories were haunting him.

"Hey, it's OK." Christa rested her hand on the side of his face. "We'll do what we can."

****

Christa sat on the far side of the room, curled up in a chair and opened a children's book she'd surreptitiously picked from Mary's bookshelf. She kept her head down when a small body wriggled in next to her.

A tiny finger pointed at the picture of Cinderella.

"Principessa."

"Yes, she's a princess." The child chattered away, completely losing Christa. She risked taking hold of Isabella's hand, moving her finger as she pointed to Cinderella's hair and details of the dress and telling her the English words as they went, finishing up with, "beautiful".

The girl's face lit up.

"Beautiful – bello."

Christa reached into her bag and drew

out a small bottle. She made a performance of opening the bottle and smelling the soft floral perfume before holding it out to Isabella. The girl took a cautious sniff and giggled. Christa said the word bagno, which she hoped meant bath, and Isabella nodded and dragged Christa to her feet.

"Vince." Christa murmured. "Does she have pajamas or a nightgown?"

He nodded and pointed to an open door behind them.

"That's her bedroom. Sarah fixed it up for her. All her clothes are there."

After a lot of splashing, giggling and a terrible effort on Christa's part to sing "Somewhere Over The Rainbow" they were done. Isabella was transformed and her jet-black curls fell gently to her shoulders, the stained dress replaced with soft pink and white flowery pyjamas.

Christa led her back into the other room and with a shy smile Isabella stepped towards Vince, then stopped short as if she didn't have the courage to go any closer. He murmured something in Italian before holding out his arms. Slowly she crept into his hug and let him hold her.

Christa turned to meet Dan's glassy eyes and they watched Isabella snuggle into Vince's neck.

"It's time we went," Dan whispered.

Vince spoke to Isabella before turning to them.

"I've told her it's bedtime. Better start as I mean to go on."

Isabella pulled away and ran across the room, chattering rapidly and throwing herself at Christa's legs.

"She's thanking you and wants to make sure you're coming to play again tomorrow. I'll tell her you will – if that's OK?" A brief flash of panic crossed Vince's face.

"Of course."

"Thanks. Come for coffee in the morning." Christa lowered her voice.

"You might want to sleep in the room with her in case she wakes up in the night."

He nodded and swept Isabella back up into his arms.

Once they were back outside in the garden, Dan and Christa were finally on their own.

"Fancy that walk now?"

"In the dark? Aunt Mary reckoned even you couldn't be that mad. It was why she didn't believe my story," Christa declared, but he sensed her smile.

"The path is lit for guests to stroll out there after a meal and tonight it's nearly a full moon. Come on... you'll be telling the truth then when we go back."

Pulling her to him, Dan pressed a gentle

kiss on her forehead.

"You've convinced me, as usual. Do you need your cane from the car?"

"No, I think you'll take good care of me," he said with a smile.

Five minutes later, surrounded by the scent of early spring roses in the secluded arbour, they settled happily to watch the sun set. A sudden picture flashed into Dan's mind of saying goodbye to this amazing woman. He cleared his throat and struggled to focus on the here and now.

"It's been a long day, how about we head home?"

For a second he wondered if this was the right moment to speak but her smile shut him up. She'd asked for a light, holiday romance so that's what he'd give her.

He slipped his arm through hers and they walked back to the car – together for now.

****

It surprised Dan to see all the house lights all still on. As he fitted the key in the lock the door sprung open.

"Oh, I'm some glad you're back." Mary's worried eyes landed on Christa.

"Is something wrong?" Christa asked anxiously. "Nothing's up with my family is there?"

"No, love, but your mum did call to warn… somebody's come to see you and…" Her words died away as the door behind her opened and a man emerged into the hall.

Dan barely caught Christa as her legs gave way.

"Antony?" The single breathless, shocked word echoed off the walls and for a minute no-one spoke.

Running Scared

HIYA, honey, don't I get a hug after coming all this way?"

Christa caught her breath and leaned closer to Dan.

"I don't think your wife would approve."

"Oh, sweetheart, that's not a problem, so come right on over here and welcome me properly. Lynette decided she preferred being single so I'm a free man again and come to throw myself on the mercy of the only woman I've ever loved."

He flung open his arms and gave Christa a beseeching look.

"I'm sorry things didn't work out with your marriage, but I'm not interested in rekindling anything with you. You might have a short memory but I don't."

Somehow she kept her voice steady.

Dan's hand tightened around her waist.

"Aw, sweetheart. I was an idiot. I hope you'll give me a chance to prove I've changed."

"Please just get the next plane back to LA and leave me alone," Christa ordered, her voice trembling.

"I've booked into a local hotel. I'm going to woo you all over again, and this time I'll get it right. I'll leave for now but I'll be back every day until you realise I mean what I say."

With another bright smile he politely thanked Irene and Mary and left.

"So he's the reason you're here, my dear?" Mary asked.

Christa felt she'd been caught out in some huge lie and hated that they might feel she'd used them.

"Why don't we go into the kitchen? We could all do with a cup of tea and then Christa can explain things to you," Dan suggested.

Christa took a sip of tea and told the two women the whole story. Her eyes met Dan's and the empathy in their deep brown depths made her want to drop her head in her hands and weep, but she finished her story...

"So I lost my job and got the weird hair on the same day. Explains a lot, doesn't it?"

Nobody spoke and Christa wished they'd yell instead of looking so sorry for her. Dan picked up her hand and stroked her fingers, easing some of her apprehension.

"Growing up I'd heard lots of stories about you guys," Christa continued, "and always intended to visit, so when I needed to get away from LA this was the first place I thought of. I reckoned I'd take some time to figure out what to do next…"

She sucked in a deep breath.

"If you feel I've abused your friendship please tell me to leave. I'll understand. I'll hate it, but I'll understand."

Mary smiled and patted her hand.

"Don't be silly, dearie. We guessed something was wrong. Your mum didn't go into detail but she hinted you'd had problems with a boyfriend. We're pleased you came and don't want you going any time soon, unless it's what you want. I stayed single because I never found a man I could completely trust and your Antony strikes me as too clever for his own good."

"You're right, of course, but it's hard to let go when you've invested years in someone." She shook her head and sighed.

Dan got up from the table, pushing his chair back out of the way.

"I'm off to bed. See you all in the morning." He stalked out without a backward glance.

"What was all that about?" Christa frowned, and instantly received another of Mary's pitying looks.

"Don't you know?" Mary said with a wry smile. "I'd say Dan loves you and is shocked you're having second thoughts about Mr Horwath."

"Loves me? Don't be silly. And who says I'm having second thoughts about Antony? I sent him away, didn't I?"

"Sort of, dearie, but when he mentioned coming again you didn't tell him not to. Your comment about throwing away years with him didn't sound very definite either."

Christa fought to get some kind of sense into her head.

"I think tomorrow I'd better go away somewhere for a few days. Please don't tell Antony where I am when he comes around."

"What about Dan?"

It might put them in an awkward position but she needed time alone to think.

"Tell him I'll be back by the weekend."

Vince and little Isabella popped into her head but she couldn't worry about that now. She'd get to Mordros Bay somehow, maybe in the afternoon instead and keep her fingers crossed not to run into Dan.

"All right, my dear, if that's what you want." Mary got up to clear away the tea cups. Christa didn't move and hunched over the table, on the verge of tears. The older woman rested a hand on her shoulder.

"It'll be all right, you know." Christa wished she could believe her. Quickly, she got up and almost ran upstairs, closing the door behind her and flinging herself on the bed, finally giving in to tears.

****

Dan strolled into the kitchen, grabbed a slice of toast from the rack and started to pour a mug of tea.

"Isn't Christa coming down for breakfast?"

"She's not here," Mary stated firmly.

"What, she's not up yet, you mean?" He glanced up from buttering and adding marmalade to his toast and intercepted a strange glance between his aunt and grandmother.

Surely Christa wasn't in her room brooding about Antony? He'd thought about it all night and come to the conclusion he'd better apologise. He'd behaved like a juvenile but it was hard when you'd never been jealous before and that was what it was – whether he liked it or not. It'd eaten him up to see the man fawning over Christa as if he'd never broken her heart.

"Christa left very early this morning. She needed a few days away but she'll be back by the weekend."

"Oh, right, where's she gone?" That drew more weird looks his way and Dan started to get annoyed. "Is it some big secret?"

"Well, she did ask me to keep quiet about where she was."

"Even to me?" He couldn't believe she'd do this to him.

"Yes, I'm sorry."

"So she's left with Antony and didn't have the courage to tell me herself. Great." Dan tossed his toast down on the plate.

Mary gave him a reproachful glance.

"Give her more credit than that, son. I'm not to tell him where she is either. She only told me in case her family called in an emergency."

"Sorry. I should've known." He stirred his tea thoughtfully. "She didn't mention anything about seeing Vince, did she? Only we were supposed to go for coffee this morning."

"No, she didn't." Mary shook her head.

"Fine. I'm off to the gym and then to Mordros Bay. I'll be down in the village later. Christa printed off more petitions and we'd planned to take them around together so I suppose I'll do it myself."

Dan left before he could be asked any more questions about Vince. Christa wasn't the only one who needed to do some thinking. His grandmother had been suspiciously quiet this morning – he'd pick up some of her favorite dark chocolate coffee cream sweets while he was out.

There was always more than one way to skin the proverbial cat.

****

Dan sat with Vince and sensed his friend trying hard not to laugh. Isabella was in the kitchen with Sarah making biscuits so they had a few minutes alone.

"I'm no expert but you need to come up with a plan and go on the attack. If Christa knows you're fighting for her it may make all the difference if she's even considering giving this Antony another chance. You've got something good going with her, right?"

Dan squirmed.

"Sorry. I don't mean to be an…"

"Idiot?" Vince's dark eyes gleamed and Dan managed a small laugh.

"All right. I get the hint. And yes, we've got something special but I don't know exactly what it is yet. Things were going great, and we were taking things slow."

He glanced away from Vince's stare.

"Now I feel cornered. When I see her again making some sort of declaration could be the only way to stop her going back to that dreadful man, but I'm not ready and don't think she is either."

He stood up and wandered over to stare out the window, taking in the power of today's rough sea in the distance. Dan jerked back around.

"What am I going to do?"

The door was flung open and Isabella ran into the room, followed by Sarah carrying a large tray. Vince raised his eyes apologetically to Dan and swept his daughter into his lap. Dan's throat tightened to see his old friend so completely bewitched – the four-year-old beauty clearly had him wrapped around her little finger.

Sarah set the tray down on the table and started to pour freshly made coffee for the three adults.

"Isabella. Sit here and drink your juice like a good girl." She pointed to the seat between Vince and herself and the child obeyed immediately. There was an instant flash of admiration in Vince's eyes and Sarah gave a tiny smile. So that's how it was, Dan thought.

Fifteen minutes of polite conversation and Dan couldn't sit still any longer.

"I'd better be going. I've got things to do.

Thanks for the coffee, Sarah." He turned to Isabella. "Thank you. The biscuits were lovely."

The little girl burst into a wide smile, and something cracked inside Dan. What would any children he and Christa have together look like? But after his difficult childhood what could he possibly know about being a good parent? The idea was out of the question.

"I'll walk down with you." Vince jumped up. "I need to check on the lunch preparations. You OK to hold the fort, Sarah?" She agreed and he quickly told Isabella in Italian where he was going.

In the entrance hall they stopped for a moment and Dan made one last request.

"I need a favour. When Christa comes, find out where she's staying and call me, please."

"Of course." Vince didn't hesitate. "But what if she won't say? She's not stupid and she'll guess you've primed me to ask."

Dan scoffed.

"I can't believe this is you saying this. You've always been able to charm the birds from the trees."

"You have such faith in me I guess I don't have any choice." Vince commented with a wry smile.

"Snap to it, Captain," Dan joked and left.

Now he'd work on tracking her down himself. Phoning the local taxi company was top of the list – always try the obvious first.

A minute later he dared to smile again.

****

Christa hurried along the pavement, looking behind her to make sure she wasn't being followed. Some might say she was paranoid but they didn't know Antony or Dan. At least she'd had the satisfaction of getting the better of Vince.

Had Dan really thought she'd fall for his friend's smooth charm? He'd unsubtly questioned her when she visited him and Isabella, but she'd been one step ahead. Dan didn't realise how many times she'd dialled his number and hung up before it could ring. She hadn't done the same with Antony which must say something.

She strolled along the scruffy main street and checked out the few shops sandwiched in between a lot of cafés and pubs. Surfing gear, cheap souvenirs and pasty shops about covered the choices. Christa hesitated outside one of the pubs before cautiously opening the door and stepping inside.

Thankfully it was almost empty and better than she'd expected with only moderately loud music and clean tables. The young barman dragged himself away from the small wall-mounted TV showing a pool game and muttered something. Christa guessed he was asking what she wanted to drink, although couldn't be sure.

"A half of lager, please."

She chose a table back in a dimly lit corner well away from the only other customer, a heavyset middle-aged man propping up the bar. Gradually a few more people trickled in but nobody seemed to speak much, only got their drinks and watched the television.

An hour later Christa was ready to admit defeat. Staring at the four walls of her hotel room would be more fascinating than this. She gathered up her jacket and bag ready to move then froze. She must be seeing things.

Antony sat at a table in the middle of the room sticking out like a sore thumb with his expensively cut, highlighted blond hair, three-hundred dollar designer ripped jeans and an Abercrombie & Fitch T-shirt – standard Los Angeles casual dress.

She stared around in panic and slunk down the narrow hallway behind her, desperate to find a back exit. There was nothing so she slipped into the ladies' bathroom.

Her heart thumped in her chest but the

sudden memory of Dan's steady hands holding her up last night, the strength he'd given without question, settled her down and she sucked in a deep breath.

In one second the questions she'd been bombarding herself with all day were answered. She would face Antony and this time every detail of the way he'd treated her for five years would be foremost in her mind.

Christa stared into the cracked, grimy mirror. Time to get this over with.

"Antony? What are you doing here? How did you find me?"

"Christa? What the…" His voice faded as he stared at her. "I came to look for you. You weren't hard to follow this morning. I'm surprised to see you hanging out in this sort of place."

Christa bristled.

"You came in here." She watched him pull himself together and his charming smile turned back on.

"Sorry, honey. Sit down and join me. Please." Antony stood and pulled out a chair for her.

Not wanting to attract too much attention from the other customers, Christa gave in and sat down.

"Antony. Let's get this over with. Last night I might have sounded unsure but it was only from shock. Now I've had time to cool off. You treated me badly for all those years and I was foolish enough to let you."

She bulldozed past his attempt to interrupt.

"I talked you into proposing because I panicked about being thirty and single which was ridiculous. You never wanted to marry me in the first place and did me a favour by cancelling the wedding – although I have to say I didn't see it at the time." She sucked in a deep breath. "Since I got here I've met someone else."

"Don't tell me, Mr Wilson, I suppose. That wasn't hard to guess. And here's me thinking I was doing you a favour by coming after you."

"Don't you dare talk to her that way. Have some respect, man." Dan's voice rang out as he crossed the room and grabbed Antony's arm.

"Let go of me." Antony tried to shake him off and Christa cried out as Dan lost his balance and crashed down on to the floor.

"Go now." She glared at Antony and reached to help Dan back up.

"Willingly." Antony strode towards the door without a backward glance.

Dan slumped down on the nearest chair, his face pale and grim. She stood over him and touched his cheek.

"I'm so sorry. Are you OK?"

"I'll live. I fell on my bad knee, that's all." He attempted to smile. "Just seeing you again makes everything better." Dan reached up to stroke her hair.

"Let's get out of this place," he insisted.

Slowly they made their way back to Dan's car and as soon as they got in he took some pain medication and drank down a whole bottle of water. He laid his head back against the seat with his eyes closed. Gradually, the colour crept back into his skin and the taut lines eased.

"Are you ready to go home?" His quiet words tugged at her heart.

Christa nodded.

"How are you going to explain away today's mishap?"

"I'll tell the truth, if that's all right with you? If it wasn't for my gran being soft I wouldn't have been there to cause trouble."

"I might've guessed you'd wheedle it out of her." Christa shook her head in mock disgust.

"Maybe you hoped she would?"

If she admitted he was right, where did that leave them? Dan took hold of her hands.

"Don't answer. Not yet."

Drama at Mordros Bay

CHRISTA closed up her phone and sighed. She'd tried to reassure her mother, but with limited success. The fact she'd finally put Antony behind her went down well, but her mother was naturally concerned about her getting friendly with another man, no matter how lovely she assured her Dan was.

"Did you get an inquisition?" Dan's deep voice rumbled in her ear and she turned around to face him.

"You could say that." Christa sighed.

As soon as she walked into the kitchen, Mary beamed at her.

"Well, my dear, I hope that's the last we've seen of the unpleasant Mr Horwath. I assume he won't be around here again any time soon?"

"I'd say so." Christa declared. "Anyway, that's enough about him. I've got an appointment at the local radio station in the morning. I'm hoping to convince them our shop protest would make an interesting story. If they agree I might get on later this week. How are the petitions going?"

Mary smiled.

"Dan brought more around the shops yesterday and collected up the others.

We've got over five hundred signatures and the tourist season will pick up next week as it is Easter, so we should get a lot more."

"Great. Has anyone heard from Pat Carhart recently? He's been suspiciously quiet."

Dan spoke up.

"Marc said Carhart hassled him one day, giving him the 'you're not a local so why do you care' line, but he sent him away with a flea in his ear. I'm afraid Emma's signed her shop over already."

Christa shrugged.

"That's no great surprise. I'll make a point to stop by and thank Marc."

****

From her place at the breakfast table his aunt threw Dan a worried glance.

"Oh, there you are, Dan. Vince called a little while ago and asked you to ring when you woke up. He sounded some worried."

"OK, will do."

"Do either of you want some breakfast?" Mary asked, glancing at Christa who'd come downstairs behind him.

"Not for me. I'll just grab a glass of juice then I need to get ready to go to the radio station." Helping herself, she quickly headed back out and Dan was left to face his aunt again.

Dan loved his family but it was long past time to make proper plans. He needed to find a job and get his own place to live – something he should have done months ago.

"Do you think Vince's problem could be something to do with the little girl staying at the hotel? You know – the one who looks exactly like him?" Mary folded her arms, sat back and waited.

"How do you…" He felt the full power of Mary's sharp eyes fixed unmercifully on him.

"Molly Pendean works in the hotel kitchen and she's an old friend of mine. She asked me up for coffee yesterday morning."

"What did Molly say?"

His aunt picked up her cup and took a sip of tea and Dan sighed and sat back down at the table. Two could play this game. He sat perfectly still.

"How long did he expect to keep a mystery daughter quiet?"

"It wasn't my secret to tell and I had to respect that."

Her eyes softened.

"I know, my love." Mary patted his hand. "Molly's a sharp woman with good ears. She heard the fuss when the grandmother arrived and afterwards when she'd gone and left the girl there. Vince has his hands full, hasn't he?"

"You could say that. He didn't know

about Isabella. He'd never have neglected his own child."

"I didn't think so for a minute, my love. What's he going to do now?"

Dan shrugged.

"Bring her up best he can, I suppose. She's a sweet kid. I'll call Vince now."

Dan glanced out of his bedroom window while he waited for Vince to answer.

"About time, Wilson, didn't you get my message?" Vince barked.

"Hey, calm down. Aunt Mary didn't say it was urgent."

"Get over here now. Please, mate." Distress throbbed in his voice and Dan's stomach gave a nasty lurch.

"What's wrong?" He crossed the fingers on his free hand.

"Isabella's disappeared. I've told the police. They're searching the cliffs." Vince's voice broke and caught on a sob.

"Hang in there. We'll find her. I promise."

Dan hung up before Vince could remind him they both had enough experience of life to know some things were in the lap of the gods.

****

A grim-faced Sarah flung open the door to Dan.

"He's upstairs with the police. Go to him. I can't seem to help." She crammed a sodden handkerchief up to her mouth and ran off towards the kitchen.

Dan trudged up the stairs and the policeman standing outside the door into Vince's private quarters glared at him.

"Captain Wilson. Here to see Mr D'Amato."

"I've orders not to let anyone in."

Suddenly the door opened.

"Get in here before I lose it." Vince grabbed Dan's elbow and dragged him inside. "Detective Inspector Garrett, he's in charge." He gestured towards a middle-aged man berating someone on the phone.

Finishing his call, the Detective Inspector turned to shake Dan's hand.

"Glad you're here. I'll bring you up to speed. Isabella asked to sleep by herself last night and went to bed at the usual time. When Mr D'Amato woke at seven this morning he went to the little girl's room but she wasn't there. He assumed she'd gone to the kitchen looking for some breakfast and went down to look for her."

He nodded towards Vince.

"No-one had seen her so the staff all helped check around the hotel and garden but didn't have any luck."

Dan put a hand on his friend's shoulders.

"He called us straight away and we've searched the building thoroughly and the garden area. Now we're widening the search." Detective Inspector Garrett's dark eyes took on a brooding aspect.

"I've got reinforcements coming and the helicopter's been called out from the naval air station."

Vince pulled from Dan's grasp.

"For God's sake let me join the search. She's my daughter!"

"You'll be a hindrance, sir. Let my men do their job. Please."

"Surely there must be something we can do?" Frustration hummed through Dan.

"The best thing you can do is support Mr D'Amato."

Dan nodded.

"You go and do what you have to and I'll stay as long as necessary."

He and Vince settled in two wing-backed chairs, one on either side of the unlit fireplace, and didn't speak for a long time.

****

Christa walked briskly from the radio station towards the bus stop, grinning to herself because it had all gone better than expected. She'd convinced the morning DJ to interview her on Thursday.

The next move was to return to Tremorva and get more information together. The station would ask Pat Carhart to come on and defend his plans, although Christa was prepared to bet he wouldn't accept.

She turned her phone back on and her message alert beeped. The first was from Robbie Wilks asking her to stop by, and after that Dan's voice came on. She tried to pay attention to what he was actually saying instead of sighing over his deep, beautiful voice like a besotted teenager.

Christa ground to a halt and the woman behind nearly walked right into her. She moved out of the way and listened to the message one more time. Through tear-filled eyes she could only watch her bus pull up, load its passengers, and leave without her.

Dan apologised for not being able to pick her up but pleaded for her to come. She hadn't a clue where to get a taxi and all she could think of was to turn around and run back towards the radio station.

Bursting back in through the front entrance she startled the receptionist.

"I was just here talking to Amy Baker – is she still around?" The girl studied her warily and Christa itched to make her hurry up.

"Is something wrong, Miss Reynolds?" Amy strolled into the foyer, nibbling on a sandwich.

"I need a favour. Well, two really. First, I need to get a taxi."

Amy smiled.

"That's easy, Jane will call you one. They're usually pretty quick." She nodded over towards the young girl. "What else can I do? Is something wrong?"

"Yeah. It's a friend of mine. His four-year-old daughter's gone missing and the police have started a search. I don't suppose you could announce on the radio for people to look out for her? The poor kid's Italian and only speaks a few words of English, although she understands more." Christa babbled and Amy gently took her arm and led her over to sit down.

"Tell me what you know. You understand I'll have to call the police before doing anything?"

Christa nodded and slowly recounted Dan's message and what she knew of Isabella. Her initial panic ebbed as Amy calmly took notes and gave the occasional brief nod. The presenter opened her phone and talked to someone, alternately telling the story and listening. She finished and lightly rested her hand on Christa's.

"They confirmed what you've told me. I'll put something together and get it on the end of the news bulletin in about ten minutes. We'll repeat it every hour until we're told to stop."

"Thanks so much. You've been great. I'm off to the hotel to see if I can help."

"Call me if there's any news." Amy passed over a business card. "That's my direct number. If I'm on air it'll roll to voicemail so leave a message and I'll get back when I can."

"The taxi's here, Miss Baker." The receptionist addressed her boss.

Christa thanked them and raced off. No car ride was ever so long and slow.

****

Vince paced up and down the room, each time stopping at the window and staring out as though he might conjure up Isabella by the power of his imagination.

Dan knew they had to do something.

"Do you want to go out for a walk and get some fresh air? I don't know about you but I'm ready to tear my hair out stuck here. We'll tell them where we're going and take our phones."

Vince agreed and Dan grabbed his cane and they headed for the door.

The easterly wind blowing in off the sea gusted in their faces and for a second they stopped, both staring towards the cliff. Dan held on to Vince's arm, feeling the strong muscles tense and shudder. They were surely both thinking the same. What hope would the little scrap of a girl stand if she'd wandered over there?

News At Last

CHRISTA shoved money at the taxi driver, probably far too much from the way he grinned, and ran across the gravel towards the hotel. A pair of strapping young policemen blocked her way to the door.

"Restaurant's closed today, miss. Better stop your taxi."

"I'm a friend of Mr D'Amato. He called earlier and asked me to come over."

"That's as may be, but we'll have to check. Give me your name and I'll call to make sure you're who you say you are."

"I'm Christa Reynolds."

He spoke her details into a radio and she blushed, hearing herself described as short, skinny, with red and blonde hair and a strong American accent. Snapping the radio shut, he almost smiled. "OK, miss. You're cleared. Mr D'Amato is…"

"Right here." Vince touched her shoulder and she swung around to meet his dark pain-filled eyes. It took all her control not to burst into tears.

"There's no news, I suppose?" Christa whispered and Vince sadly shook his head.

She forced out a smile.

"Let's go in. I could do with some coffee, I don't know about you pair." She linked arms with Dan and they headed through the main door. "You go on upstairs. I'll find Sarah and get a tray organised."

The kitchen was silent and the few staff who'd remained sat quietly around the long wooden table at the far end of the room.

"Sarah, we wondered if you would bring up a tray of coffee, please? Put an extra cup on for yourself." The young woman's grateful half-smile lifted Christa's spirits; Vince needed all the help he could get.

The moment she walked into the upstairs lounge Isabella's disappearance became horribly real at the sight of Vince, sitting on the sofa and holding his daughter's pink fluffy elephant in his large hands.

"It's all right, love, they'll find her." Dan wrapped his warm arms around her trembling shoulders.

Sarah carried in a tray of drinks and sandwiches and set it on the table. She caught Christa's eye and took a deep breath. Going over to Vince she dropped to her knees on the carpet and tentatively pulled him into her arms.

"Let's leave them alone," Dan whispered

and led Christa out. On the way downstairs he hesitated.

"Do you need something to eat or are you OK to walk awhile?"

"Let's walk. Take me to the rose arbour."

They didn't speak as they made their way slowly along the path and into the secluded spot they loved. Together they sat on the bench and Dan wrapped her in his arms. He always made her feel safe and cared for.

"Vince said Isabella wasn't very happy yesterday. She talked a lot about her grandmother and the town where they lived and cried about her mother, too. Vince promised they'd visit her grandmother soon and thought she was OK."

Christa sighed.

"Poor kid. I think we've all forgotten what she's been through. A new bedroom, pretty clothes, and a doting father don't make up for the fact her mother died and the only other person she loved abandoned her. Apart from Vince, she can't even talk much to anyone. I can't imagine what that's like."

"I can," he growled, "apart from the language thing. My mother wasn't very good at the whole parenting thing, but she was still mine and loved me. It tore me up when she died and I felt responsible. Kids aren't very logical." For a second his voice wavered.

"At least I was older when she died and had my father and Aunt Mary and Gran, so I was pretty well off compared to Isabella."

Christa made herself concentrate on Isabella, though her heart broke for Dan.

"Think what she might've done. She wants her real home. Do you think she's old enough to make plans to leave?"

"She's a determined little soul, so, yes, I do, but there's no bus stop near here and I doubt Isabella knows much about English money yet. If she'd walked away she couldn't have got far."

Christa told him about the radio announcements.

"That's great." His cheerful tone didn't fool her for a second. "I guess we'd better go back."

They walked slowly back to the hotel, dreading the idea of facing Vince again if there wasn't any good news.

****

"Is there any coffee left?" Christa asked as she walked back in and Vince moved his arm from Sarah's shoulders.

"Yes, of course." Sarah picked up the carafe and poured them some.

"Guess what I did this morning?" Christa chatted about her visit to the radio station, hoping to ease the tension for a minute.

At the sound of voices outside the door Vince half rose from the sofa. Detective Inspector Garrett strode in and lifted his hand to stop any questions.

"Don't get too excited, but we think we've found Isabella safe."

Vince jumped to his feet.

"What do you mean, don't get excited?"

"We've had a call from a reliable lady who says Isabella's turned up at her house." He gestured towards Dan. "Your gran called and described the girl she found. I don't think there are any other black-haired, Italian-speaking four-year-olds wandering around, but I could be wrong."

He allowed a smile in Vince's direction.

"Come with me, sir, and we'll go straight to the house."

"We'll follow in my car." Dan announced.

Vince took hold of Sarah's hand.

"Come with me, please."

Hot tears fell unchecked down Christa's cheeks and Dan wrapped her in an all-encompassing hug while one of his large hands rubbed her back.

"How on earth did she get to your house?" Christa couldn't make any sense of this turnaround.

"I haven't the foggiest idea, but I'm glad she did." Dan's voice roughened. "Come on, love, let's go."

****

"Papa?" Isabella whispered.

Vince's fluent Italian was unintelligible to everyone else in the room, but the meaning was perfectly clear as he replied in loving tones. He swept his daughter into his arms and held on.

"When she's ready we need to find out how she got here, but that'll wait. She needs to be checked out by a doctor, too."

"I'll get Doctor Morton to come up to the hotel and have a look at her this afternoon." Vince cradled his daughter on his lap, frowning with worry. "Can I take her home now?"

The Inspector willingly agreed.

"Mrs Treneague, I hope you don't mind but we need to ask you a few questions."

From her chair Irene spoke up.

"I understand perfectly." She smiled at the policeman. "Do you need me to come to the police station?"

"We can chat here for now, but you'll need to come in to sign your statement unless it's difficult for you and we can make other arrangements."

"I'm perfectly able to come there."

Dan stifled a smile at her enthusiasm.

"Do you mind if we go into your kitchen? I'll bring PC Dana Barnes in to take notes if that's OK?" Garrett nodded to the young blonde policewoman waiting by the door.

"Follow me." Irene rose and graciously led the way.

"We're going back to Mordros Bay. You coming?" Vince asked Dan.

"Not now. You take care of Isabella and we'll stop by later." He gave an easy smile.

With Isabella snuggled in his arms Vince left, accompanied by a smiling Sarah.

"I'd say this is a successful day all around." Christa wound her arms around Dan's neck and gave him a brilliant smile that made his heart sing.

"What are the police doing here?" Mary burst into the room, glaring at them both.

"Gran found little Isabella here earlier."

"Here? Is she all right?" Worry etched deep lines in her face.

"She's fine. We don't know how she got here. Gran fell asleep and woke up to find Isabella standing in front of her."

"Where's Mother now?" Mary looked anxiously around.

"She's in the kitchen giving a statement and loving every minute." Dan gave a reassuring smile.

"When they're finished, how about Christa and I fix supper? We told Vince we'd go over later to see how he is, but we won't stay long." He noticed an extra layer of tiredness clouding his aunt's usual cheer. "Was the café busy today?" he asked.

She shook her head.

"Not really. Pat Carhart came in earlier bothering me to sign his stupid agreement. You'd have been proud of me. I told him where to go in quite unladylike terms."

The Inspector stuck his head back around the door.

"We'll be gone now. If you could bring your grandmother up to the station in the morning I'd appreciate it. I'll make sure to have tea and a tour lined up for her." He grinned, instantly younger and less strained.

Dan made his way to the kitchen.

"I don't know about anyone else but I'm starving. Come on." He grabbed Christa's hand and dragged her with him.

"How about omelettes and salad?"

"Perfect."

Dan smiled, thinking they were back on an even keel for now and hoping it'd last.

A Sad Decision

SARAH welcomed them with a smile.

"Come on up, Isabella's fast asleep and Vince has a bottle of champagne on ice waiting for us – typical, isn't it?

"Pour the drinks, love, we need to celebrate," Vince ordered with a smile.

Christa couldn't stamp on her curiosity any longer.

"First tell us what the doctor said and then catch us up with what Isabella said about how she ended up in Tremorva."

"She's a journalist, Vince, sorry." Dan gave Christa's hair a gentle muss and laughed.

Vince took a sip of champagne.

"She can't help it. Doctor Morton said Isabella's fine apart from being tired. You'll never believe the rest. The little girl's a lot smarter than we gave her credit for. For a start she's soaked up a lot more English than we realised."

It didn't surprise Christa, people generally underestimated children.

"She wanted to get back to Italy and had the idea you'd help."

"Me? But I've never said anything..."

"I know," he cut her off, "but somehow she got it into her head. Isabella spent a lot of time in the kitchen and they'd talk a lot, thinking she couldn't understand. Molly Pendean mentioned living in Tremorva and visiting her friend Mary. Isabella worked out that Mary was in Dan's family and knew you lived at his house so put it all together."

Dan shook his head in disbelief.

"The clever little creature."

"She saw Molly leave work every night in her car so last night after I'd put her to bed she crept downstairs and hid. When Molly parked outside her house Isabella crept out. It was dark by then so she…"

Vince's voice broke and it took him a minute to compose himself.

"She hid in the unlocked garden shed and curled up on some old rugs and slept."

There was complete silence as they all wondered what could have happened.

"This morning she walked into the village and somehow found the right house. Isabella watched you both leave then sneaked in the back door and hid behind the living-room curtains. Your gran went in after lunch to listen to the radio and Isabella heard her name on the news.

"They pronounced it wrong so she popped out and complained. Completely shocked your gran, of course. Thank goodness you set up the radio announcements."

Vince squeezed Christa's hand, unable to say any more.

"I'm only glad it helped." Christa took a deep breath. Dan would tell her not to interfere but she couldn't stay silent.

"You know you have to sort this out when she's recovered, don't you? She can't do this again."

126

Vince's expression darkened.

"Yes. I know. I'm planning to take a couple of weeks off and take Isabella back to Veroncella for a visit. I hope then she'll understand this is her home now." He took Sarah's hand in his. "With us."

Dan stood up.

"We'd better get off now. It's been a long day and Gran and Aunt Mary will want to hear all this. I assume you're OK with it being all around the village tomorrow?"

"I couldn't deprive them of the pleasure or I'd never get any of your aunt's cake again and life wouldn't be worth living."

Vince laughed and shooed them out.

****

Dan cornered Christa as she headed to bed.

"How about a walk?"

She glanced away, unable to meet his warm smiling eyes.

"Not tonight, Dan. It's been a long day."

"What's up?"

The memory of Vince, Sarah, and Isabella wouldn't leave her mind. She played for time.

"I need to think some more."

"What about?"

Christa hesitated.

"Us? Where we're headed. I mean we're

good friends and everything, but..." Her voice trailed away.

"Then what's the problem?"

"I'm pretty certain I want more," she said quietly.

Dan's smile disappeared and her heart clenched as he stroked a finger down her cheek.

"I thought we understood each other," Dan said gently. "I've got to decide what to do with the rest of my life before I can plan anything else, and I thought after Antony you felt the same. Did I get it wrong?"

She shook her head.

"You were right, but things have changed, at least for me they have."

"I'm sorry. I never meant to hurt you."

Christa cleared her throat.

"I know and it's not your fault. People change." She pulled away from his touch. "Will you do me one favour?"

"Of course, what is it?"

"Tell Aunt Mary and your gran. Maybe you can say it was just a holiday romance and we're still good friends."

"All right." He hesitated. "But..."

She stepped forward and put her fingers over his mouth.

"Don't say any more. Please. I can't bear it. I'll move out tomorrow and find somewhere else to stay until I'm done with the shop campaign."

"Fine. Good night." He walked away.

Christa wrapped her hands around herself and clung on tight, anything to stop her following the man she loved more than anything. She'd get no sleep tonight. How she'd get through the rest of the days before returning home Christa had no idea.

* * * *

Dan glared at the table and pushed his breakfast around the plate. Nobody had mentioned Christa yet but he felt two sets of eyes boring into him. He pushed his chair back and took his dishes over to the sink. He breathed steadily for a minute, then turned to his gran and aunt before he lost his nerve.

"Things haven't worked out with me and Christa but we're still friends. She doesn't feel comfortable staying her so she'll move out as soon as she finds another room, but plans to continue to help with the shops protest so you'll still see her."

Irene shook her head sadly.

"I'm sorry, my boy. I know you really…"

Mary touched her mother's hand.

"It's probably for the best. I might be able to suggest some places for her to try."

She began to clear the table.

"What are your plans for the day, Dan?"

"I'm going up to London for a few days. I've got some business to sort out and it's time I saw my father." A dose of Jonathan Wilson's commonsense was exactly what he needed after he'd apologised for being a thoughtless son. It would get him away from Christa, too – a decided bonus.

"Give our regards to Jonathan. Does he know you're coming?" Mary scrutinised him closely and Dan shook his head.

"Not yet. I've only now made up my mind, but I've been considering it for a while. I'll throw a few things in a bag then I'll be off and leave my car up at the station. Call my mobile if you need anything."

Dan made a quick escape before they could ladle on any more sympathy.

****

Christa heard Dan's heavy footsteps on the stairs and cowered behind her closed door. Hopefully, he'd leave soon so she could escape and head off to see Robbie Wilks about his message and find out whether he knew of a room to rent.

She held her breath until she heard Dan go back downstairs. A minute later the front door closed with his distinctive slam. Cautiously, she crept down herself and almost succeeded in sneaking out.

"Good morning." Mary's sharp voice startled her.

"Oh… Hi. I was…"

"I just wanted to say how sorry I am that you're leaving," Mary said, frowning. "But if you've made up your mind, I'll help you find somewhere to stay," she added.

"Thanks," Christa said. "I'm real sorry how things turned out. I hope you still want help with the shops?"

Mary's face softened.

"Of course, my love. If you find somewhere I'll take you in the car with all your things."

Christa's eyes prickled with unshed tears.

"You're very kind. I didn't want to have to ask Dan."

"He's not here. He's gone to London."

"Oh, really, was that planned?" She bit her tongue wishing she'd kept quiet.

"I'm not sure." Mary replied, not quite meeting Christa's eyes.

"Fair enough. I'll see you later." With a quick goodbye she made her escape.

****

"Hello there, lovely lady. What have I done to have my day brightened with your divine presence?" Robbie jumped up from behind the counter and flashed a smile.

His warm reception cheered Christa.

"Two things. You left a message saying you had some info for me. Sorry I took so long getting back to you but I was up at Mordros Bay."

"Don't fret." He brushed away her concern. "Is the kid all right?"

"Yeah, thank goodness."

"I wanted to let you know I found out that Pat Carhart's younger brother, Ivan, isn't pleased with the plan and he's working on their mother to influence him. Apparently she's wavering slightly." He grinned, plainly satisfied with himself.

"Wow, that's huge."

Wheels spun in Christa's head as she considered her next move.

"If I wanted to speak to the mother and brother without Pat around where do I find them?"

"They live in a big house at the top of Polmear Hill. Today's Tuesday, and Pat always goes to his Rotary Club meeting at seven so there's a good chance you'll find the others at home alone. Would you like me to come with you?"

She guessed the Carharts might be more responsive with someone local.

"All right, thanks."

"What's the next problem you need

sorted, Cinderella? Tell your handsome prince and I'll see what I can do."

She couldn't help responding to his mischievous smile.

"I need a room or flat to rent. I don't suppose you know anywhere?"

"I might do." His eyes darkened as he sized her up. "I don't mean to be nosey, but why the move? I thought you were being well looked after by our local war hero," he teased and she hesitated over how to reply.

"Dan and I are friends, nothing more. Once I'm done with the shops protest it's back to California for me."

"As it happens I've the perfect solution. This flat's got three bedrooms and my mother lives here with me so that leaves one spare and ready for a guest."

"Wow, that'd be great. I'd be happy to give it a try if you are. Mary offered to help move my things so we'll do that after work if it's OK?"

Robbie grinned.

"I can do better than that. I take my lunch from one to two so we can pick up your stuff then, if you'd like?"

"That'd be better. I'll go to the café and let Mary know and then head on back to the house. Do you mind meeting me there?"

"No problem. See you at one. By the way, do you surf?"

"Surf? Yeah, course I do. Why?"

"We could go over to Fistral beach one night. It's the best one around."

"I don't see why not." Apart from how much it'd hurt Dan if he found out. She hardened her heart.

"I'd better sort my things out. See you later."

She breezed out before she could change her mind.

No Going Back?

DAN slipped off his sunglasses and stared up at Wilson Enterprises, his father's domain. The multi-storey building always intimidated him and today was no different.

His stomach tightened and he wondered what sort of reaction he'd get. He headed inside before he could change his mind and stopped at the security desk in the lobby.

"Mr Wilson. This way, please."

An elegant raven-haired woman led him up in the elevator towards the penthouse suite where Jonathan reigned over his empire.

Dan stood awkwardly in the doorway. The huge office with its modern furnishings, exotic plants, and priceless artwork on the walls were perfectly calculated to intimidate and his heart raced.

Jonathan was leaning back in an oversized black leather chair, his shirtsleeves rolled up and his feet resting on the edge of the imposing black walnut desk. Dan knew better than to take the apparent casualness at face value – it was cover for a very shrewd, smart man.

His apology, rehearsed over and over on the long train journey, evaporated and he slowly crossed the room until he stood directly in front of the desk. He stood, feet slightly apart, hands by his side and waited.

In his usual unhurried way his father stood, strolled around the desk and fixed his piercing blue eyes on him.

"You're looking good. You've made me wait a long time to say that."

Dan's throat tightened.

"I'm sorry." His father pulled him into a tight embrace and held on tight before easing back and staring at his errant son.

"I hope you're staying a while?"

"A couple of days at least. I'm off to get a hotel room now but I'll come over to see you tonight, if that's all right?"

"Don't be an idiot, Daniel, you'll stay at the house. I'll rearrange a few things and we'll talk over dinner."

"You don't have to if you've plans." Dan stumbled over his words.

"I'm perfectly aware of that, but don't argue. I'll call and tell them to expect you. I should be there by seven."

Dan was dismissed and quickly made his escape. Coming here got him away from Christa, but Jonathan would make sure it wasn't an easy option.

****

"We're fine, Dan. The weather's good and we've lots of visitors around. Was the train bad?" Mary was never happy when anyone she loved travelled far. "How's Jonathan? Tell him it's too long since he's visited us and get him to take a break from that nasty, dirty city."

Dan smiled to himself and lay back on the bed.

"He's doing well. I'll pass on your message."

"I'll tell you, so you don't have to ask. Christa moved out at lunchtime."

"Already? Where's she gone?"

Silence. Mary plainly didn't want to say.

"Did she ask you not to tell me?" Dan demanded.

"No, dear, it's… well… she's renting a room in Robbie Wilks's flat over his shop."

The words struck him hard.

"You're joking?"

"No, I wouldn't do that, my love. He offered his spare room so I suppose it was easier than looking around any more."

The small pocket of hope he'd kept alive, that maybe they'd work things out, shrivelled and died.

"Oh, well, I guess that's it then."

"Don't you go reading too much into this. His mother lives with him, you know, and he's just friendly to everyone, it's his way. I thought you'd a better opinion of her?"

"I do," he said grudgingly. "Anyway, she's free to do what she wants."

"Exactly. And you didn't want to make any promises, not that I blame you after only a few weeks, but you can't expect her to sit around and wait for you to have second thoughts."

Dan needed to change the subject before he said something stupid.

"You're right. Look, I've got to go now, Auntie. I need to change for dinner – you know what Jonathan's like. I'll let you know when I'm getting back. Bye."

He quickly ended the conversation.

He should get on and shower but instead he ached to hop on the next train back to Cornwall and snatch Christa away, tell her how stupid he'd been, and plead with her to give him another chance.

Instead, he limped into the bathroom. Jonathan would read his mood like a book, as he always did.

He was in for a fun evening.

****

Chrissie's mouth gaped open as Robbie strolled into the kitchen. The casual surfer clothes were replaced by crisply ironed khaki trousers and a blue open-necked

138

dress shirt. His tanned feet were encased in black Italian leather shoes instead of their usual flip-flops, and the blond, shiny hair was tied back in a neat ponytail.

"Mrs Carhart doesn't appreciate my wild ways, and I don't want to put her back up straight away," he explained with a smile.

"I appreciate you making the effort."

Robbie held out his arm.

"If you're ready, we'll go."

Talk about from the frying pan into the fire.

* * * *

Everything about Mrs Carhart was daunting; from her chiselled-face, and rigid grey hair, to the way she sat perfectly upright in her wing-back chair with her hands neatly folded in her lap.

"What do you think of your eldest son's plans regarding the shops on Bridge Street? There's a lot of concern in the village."

Christa perched on the edge of the chair and tried not to show her awkwardness.

"We appreciate they belong to your family," Robbie intervened with a smile, "but I know a fair-minded lady like yourself appreciates these shops have been part of the local community for generations."

The older woman's face softened a little.

Christa smiled inwardly, knowing even this fierce woman wasn't immune to Robbie's charm.

"Well, young man, I know your dear mother was a good friend of mine, but I can't see what it's got to do with this... outsider." She threw a look of complete disdain in Christa's direction. "I defer to Pat for business decisions since my husband's passing and he's given this a lot of thought. Of course I'm sorry for the shopkeepers." Margaret Carhart's hands clenched tightly together. "In most cases you're people I've known all my life and it distresses me, but Pat assures me it's too good a business opportunity to pass up."

Ivan Carhart's long, thin face and hooded dark eyes came to life and he leaned in to take hold of his mother's hands.

"Don't upset yourself. Why don't I have a word with Pat and tell him how we feel?"

Margaret Carhart stared at her youngest son as though she'd forgotten he was there.

"I'd have thought you'd learned by now it's a waste of your time and breath."

She turned back to Robbie.

"I'm sorry, Mr Wilks, but I'm not prepared to interfere. If Ivan wishes to get involved, naturally that's up to him."

She fixed a hard stare at him and Ivan's gaze dropped away and every line of his body tensed.

"I expect you can find your own way out." Mrs Carhart dismissed them with a slight inclination of her head.

Christa tried to gather up her senses, wanting only to get out of there unscathed. Outside the front door, Ivan hurried towards them, thrust a business card in her hand, and ventured a brief smile.

"I couldn't say any more in there, for obvious reasons." He rolled his eyes in his mother's direction. "I want to help, but can't be publicly involved, not yet anyway. Contact me and we'll talk."

He disappeared and left them staring at each other.

They didn't venture another word until they were safely away from Polmear House.

"How about a drink?" Robbie asked. "I think we deserve one after that little exhibition. At least we know where they stand and we've got Ivan on our side."

"But he doesn't want anyone to find that out, so how does it help us?"

"I'm pretty sure he could be persuaded to share what he knows of Pat's plans if we play him right. Think smart."

Christa's unease grew.

"Couldn't that be tricky?"

"You want to save the shops, don't you?" Robbie's silvery eyes fixed on her.

"Of course."
There was no going back now.

****

Jonathan pushed back from the dinner table and offered Dan a cigar, but he shook his head.

"Turned into one of the anti-smoking brigade, have you?"

"You know I never touched it much, it wasn't hard to quit." He didn't admit he hadn't touched a cigarette since Christa arrived.

"Doesn't bother me if you carry on."

"How gracious of you." Jonathan's dry sarcasm made Dan smile. He lit his cigar and waited until he'd taken a couple of puffs before speaking again. "So, who's the woman who's got to you?"

"What do you mean?" He vacillated, putting off the inevitable. "I needed to apologise to you and…"

Jonathan waved a hand dismissively.

"I appreciate all that, but you might as well admit a problem with a woman drove you here today. Tell me about her."

Dan slumped back into the chair. His father could be the consummate diplomat, but he'd made his fortune knowing when to swoop in for the kill.

"Her name's Christa Reynolds and she's an American journalist. She'd lost her job and had a broken engagement so needed a break from Los Angeles. Her grandmother was evacuated with the Treneague's during the war so she had the idea to pay a visit. We were friends for a while, and now we're not."

Dan fiddled with the stem of the brandy glass.

His father raised one eyebrow and drawled out a long, slow, "Really."

"Yes, really." Dan was good at waiting people out, but his father was a genius. "Fine. So I still care for her, OK. We had an agreement — at least I thought we did."

"Don't tell me she mentioned the dreaded word."

Dan didn't have a clue what Jonathan was getting at.

"Commitment, dear boy, commitment. What women want and too many men run a mile from. Women civilize us and make life worth living, but we're stubborn creatures."

Dan's nerves jangled.

"If it's so great, why have you stayed single since Mum died?"

Pouring them both another drink, Jonathan took a deep swallow of his own before answering.

"That's a good question. I've never told you how I met your mother, have I?"

"You don't have to." Dan wished he'd kept quiet.

"Yes, I do. You deserve to know. I was barely eighteen when I met Lizzy, and she was the most gorgeous girl I'd ever seen." He paused. "I met her at a friend's party. I'd never had a girlfriend before and fell head over heels in love. She fascinated me because she was so different from the sort of girls I usually met."

"You mean she was your brush with ordinary?"

"Don't you ever call your mother ordinary," Jonathan snapped. "She was a smart girl and could've been anything. Life conspired against her in many ways, and I was one of them. I loved her, as far as a young boy can.

"I talked her into marrying me against my parents' wishes. They wanted me to graduate before I settled down. Once we were married they came around and helped us out, especially when we had you."

He shook his head sadly.

"Neither of us was ready to be parents but we tried. Lizzie often used to take you down to Cornwall, although she always felt stifled there and would be relieved to come back."

"I always loved it there. It seemed... steadier in a way." Dan tried to explain, meeting Jonathan's sad eyes.

"You never complained, you were a stoic little boy, and I should've realised how tough it was on you. I was so focused on my career and making money I didn't make time for my family and it's my only regret."

Dan touched his father's arm.

"You did your best after we lost Mum." He wasn't sure it was true, but Jonathan had clearly beaten himself up enough.

"One of the main reasons I sent you away to school was because you looked so much like Lizzy it hurt to see you every day. That was wrong of me."

There was no right answer to give so Dan stayed silent.

"I've remained single," Jonathan continued, "because I was too scared to marry again, afraid I wouldn't get it right. No-one's touched my heart the way Lizzy did and being your father is more than enough for me."

Dan fought against the tears pricking his eyes. Was he repeating his father's mistakes?

"If you've got something worthwhile with Christa don't let her get away. You may not get another chance."

Standing up, Dan gave his father a hug.

"Thanks, for everything."

****

The next day they met up again in the evening and sipped wine together on the patio, enjoying an unusually mild spring evening.

"I might stay a few more days if that's OK?" Dan asked, pleased at the smile his question brought to his father's face.

"Of course. You're not in any hurry to get back to Cornwall then?"

Dan's expression clouded.

"Not really. I was helping with the shops protest, but I don't think they'll miss me. I'll ring Aunt Mary later." He nibbled on another olive.

"I have to say you're moving well these days. By those muscles I assume you work out?" He gestured towards Dan's arms.

"I'm as fit as I'll get. Later on I'll probably get arthritis in this leg, but there's not much to be done about that. I can't run or walk long distances, but I'm better off than a lot."

"It's taken you a while to say that, hasn't it?"

Dan almost smiled, more pleased than he had a right to be. Maybe he was getting somewhere after all.

"Yes," he admitted.

"I'm glad to hear it. Means you're ready

to move on." Jonathan gave him a questioning look. "I've got many different business interests and you've got a sharp brain and plenty of experience working with a wide range of people. I could use you."

Dan wasn't sure how to phrase his reservations without hurting his father's feelings.

"Thanks. I'll think about it."

"What else have you considered? I suspect it's nothing to do with property acquisition and development," Jonathan teased.

"I want to help other wounded veterans. There's a ton of official rehabilitation courses, but I resented all that and I'm not the only one. I've a vision of something which tailors the help more individually. Cornwall's simple and rugged, it'd be perfect." He couldn't resist a smile, out in the open it didn't sound totally crazy.

Jonathan gave a shrewd nod.

"You've thought this through pretty well, haven't you?"

"Sort of. I'd need backing, though, and I don't want you to think the only reason I came is to…" Dan's skin heated with embarrassment. "I'm planning to visit a few banks tomorrow."

His father gave a wry smile.

"What are families for? I'm not going to

hand you the money on a plate, but if you come up with a decent business plan I'll give you an interest-free loan for as much as you need."

Emotion tightened Dan's throat, making it difficult to speak.

"Thanks. When I return to Cornwall I'll search for a good spot and sort out more details before I get back to you. I appreciate your help more than I…"

Jonathan brushed away his attempt at thanks.

At least running away from Christa achieved something Dan had craved for a long time – reconciliation and understanding with his father. This was the silver lining in the middle of his abject misery over messing up what could've been the best thing ever in his life. Dan only wished it made him feel better.

Two's Company

CHRISTA pondered what to wear, which was ridiculous. Who cared what you wore on the radio? She'd stayed up late the night before preparing answers to every question Amy Baker could possibly come up with.

Banging sounds from the kitchen reminded her Robbie was around.

She picked up the Cornish pisky ornament from her dresser, gazed into its amber eyes and desperately wished she'd given it to Dan before they parted. Maybe it would've given him a clue to how she felt. But then again, she was pretty sure he knew her thoughts and had run from them.

If she had any sense she'd return to California now and get on with her life.

"You're going to miss the bus," Robbie yelled.

"I'm coming." Christa collected her things and ran out to the other room.

"I'll be opening up soon. Good luck." Robbie said with a smile.

"Remember to phone in some intelligent questions."

"There are a few people around here who'd never use my name and the word intelligent in the same sentence."

Christa sensed a touch of hurt behind his laughter but smiled along with him.

"Don't worry, I'll ring," he assured her.

"Thanks. I must dash."

* * * *

In the radio station Christa attempted to discreetly wipe away the sheen of sweat forming on her skin. Answering questions instead of asking them was the pits. Amy

Baker couldn't be nicer, but this was the most nerve-wracking thing she'd ever had to endure. Thank goodness Pat Carhart turned down the offer to appear or even give a statement.

She held her breath and waited for the audience questions to start.

"Our first caller is Daniel Wilson."

No! It must be someone else with the same name.

"Everyone in the village appreciates what you're doing, Miss Reynolds. My family's been in business there for eighty years and we're hoping for eighty more. Mr Carhart needs to realise the village is against him and that community is more important than profit."

Hearing Dan's steady, true voice, Christa was speechless.

Amy jumped in when she didn't react.

"Thanks for calling, Mr Wilson. Miss Reynolds will respond after our next break." Turning on the adverts she switched her microphone off.

"What's up? You need to speak to him when we're back on."

A deep blush flooded Christa's face.

"I'm sorry. I hadn't expected to hear from that person, that's all."

The break didn't last nearly long enough. Christa sucked in a deep breath.

"Dan, thanks for calling. Let's hope Mr Carhart's listening and realises he's got a fight on his hands."

"Now to our next caller." Amy switched to another line. "Robbie, you're on."

"I'm another of the threatened shopkeepers and a huge supporter of Christa. My message to Mr Carhart is that even members of his own family have their qualms about this scheme and some are supporting our campaign. What's your next move, Christa, or is it top secret?"

She'd strangle him if he was here. Ivan Carhart wouldn't speak to them again if he heard Robbie's stupid comment, let alone help in any way.

"I think we should take the Carhart family's comments with a grain of salt. As to my plans I'm hoping we can get on local television and spread our message to a wider audience. We'll push harder on our petition and arrange a demonstration in the village to show how widespread our support is.

Amy disconnected him and went to the other open line, giving Christa the chance to get her scrambled brain back in some kind of working order. She'd never been so glad for something to end. Amy put on some music and eased off her headphones.

"I think that went well, don't you?"

"Yeah, really great, and thanks for inviting me. Any chance of doing an update in a few weeks? If you could pass on any feedback you get that'd be cool."

"I'd be happy for you to return, and of course I'll let you know what I hear back."

Christa said goodbye and left, virtually collapsing on the nearest empty bench outside. She took out her phone and stared hard at it. Hearing Dan's voice again had undone her.

The loud ring tone made her jump.

"Hey, you did great." Robbie's warm voice came down the line. "Carhart should be quivering in his boots."

"No thanks to you. You must've been mad to mention the whole family thing!"

"It's bound to come out sooner or later and I figured rattling Ivan's cage might do the trick. If we stay inside the box we're done for and you know it." Robbie declared and she sighed heavily.

"Yeah, I guess you're right." Christa hesitated a second.

"And yes, I did hear Dan. You sounded surprised."

"I thought with him being in London…"

"I'm sure he wanted to give his support despite the fact you two broke up," Robbie carried on. "Why don't we have dinner out somewhere nice later to celebrate your publicity triumph and plan the next move?"

"I'm not sure." Now she was being silly.
"All right, that'll be good. I'm going to
hang around here a while and do some
shopping. I'll be back later this afternoon."

She hung up but didn't move
immediately. What would happen if she
called Dan to thank him for phoning in, or
was he waiting for her to do exactly that?

She'd go shopping for some pretty
clothes then go out with Robbie – a little
friendly company was harmless, wasn't it?

****

Christa's heart flipped unpleasantly as
Robbie braked hard on the rough gravel
driveway. He'd been coy about where they
were going and now she understood why.

"I haven't been here for ages but the
food's always great," he said lightly, but she
couldn't quite meet his eyes.

"Yes, I know."

Robbie ran around to open her door.

"Come on, let's treat ourselves."

She smiled and stepped out, wondering
how she'd get through this.

"Welcome to Mor…" Sarah's words
drifted away as her wide-eyed gaze swept
over them both.

"Hi, Sarah. Do you know Robbie Wilks?

He owns the surf shop in Tremorva. We're in need of some of your awesome food."

The professional in Sarah took over and she ushered them in. Their table was tucked behind a pillar, not one of the prime spots.

Robbie chatted easily about business, the weather and her radio interview, and was seemingly oblivious to her lack of response. It was torment to look across the table at him because all her mind saw was Dan's warm smile when they were here together.

"Good evening, Christa. I hope you both enjoyed your dinner?"

Vince's deep voice startled her into dropping her coffee spoon.

"It was wonderful as always." She flashed a bright smile and introduced Robbie who received nothing but a stiff handshake.

"How's Isabella?" Christa searched for something innocuous to talk about.

"She's well, thank you. We're going to Italy next week, but when we return I know she'd love to see you again."

She didn't respond straightaway and Robbie interrupted, "I think we'd better be going, Christa." Vince excused himself and Christa went out to the entrance hall while Robbie disappeared off to the men's room.

Suddenly Vince appeared next to her and grasped hold of her elbow.

"You surprise me, Christa." His voice was

dark with anger. "What about Dan?"

Her face flamed.

"Not that it's any of your business but we aren't a couple any more. Ask Dan for the details and I'm sure you'll sympathise with his explanation."

"I do apologise." The usual smoothness returned and he flashed a brief smile. "Please excuse my bad manners. I'm glad you enjoyed your meal and look forward to welcoming you again very soon."

Robbie strolled back out and Christa quickly snatched hold of his hand, not letting go until they were at the car.

****

Dan entered Vince's number before he could come to his senses.

"Hey, how's it going?" He launched into the story of seeing his father and the new plans he was considering but Vince didn't have much to say.

"OK, what's up?" Dan asked. "There's nothing wrong with Isabella is there?"

"No, she's great. We're off to Veroncella on Monday."

"Oh, right. I'm not coming back until Tuesday. Jonathan's having a party at his country house and he's talked me into staying."

Vince hooted.

"Mixing with the elite now, are we?"

"You know what, D'Amato? You've been stuck in Cornwall so long it's rotted your brain, such as it is." Dan changed his tone. "So what's the problem? Don't you think my rehab idea's feasible?"

"Yes, it sounds great. It's not that. I…"

"I suppose you've seen Christa." Dan sighed. "Did she come to see Isabella?"

"No. She was here for dinner."

Dan didn't really want to know the answer to his next question.

"Who with?"

"Robbie from the surf shop," Vince said.

"It figures. She wanted to move after we split and he offered her his spare room." Dan struggled to keep going, but it was as if he had to punish himself for being daft. "How did she look?"

"Good. She was dressed up in some sort of pretty red dress. She did grab hold of Robbie's hand when they walked out, but that was after I'd had a go at her, so that might have been defiance."

Dan's throat tightened.

"You didn't have to defend me, you know."

"I didn't. I asked what was up between you two and she told me to ask you."

Vince waited and Dan choked out a brief

version of their final meeting.

"You sad creature," Vince snorted.

"A little sympathy would've been acceptable."

"Yeah, well, before Isabella came and I realised my feelings for Sarah I might've given you some, but things are different now. When Isabella ran away it shook me out of my complacency.

"I want better for the rest of my life and so should you. It's obvious you and Christa are made for each other and you know it. The trouble is by the time you come to your senses it might be too late."

"I'll see you when you get back. Have a great time with Issy. Is Sarah going, too?"

"I wish she could but I need her here at the hotel to keep things running smoothly. Maybe you could look in on her occasionally to see if there's anything she needs."

Dan agreed without hesitation and they finished the conversation. He wasn't sure it'd done him much good.

The Waiting Game

DAN stepped off the train and stood for a moment to savour the soft, warm air. No outpost of Wilson Enterprises was half this lovely. His father was welcome to city life.

Dan's good mood lasted through the drive to Tremorva until he pulled up outside the house and grasped the steering wheel, fighting down memories of Christa. He'd walk inside and put on a smile. Aunt Mary and his gran had worried about him enough recently and as long as he didn't look directly into their eyes he might be OK.

"There you are. Get yourself in and see Gran. Tea's ready. I made us some small pasties for a treat. I bet you haven't had anything decent for days." Mary swept him into a warm hug and shooed him inside.

After he'd finished eating, Dan told them about his visit and his business plans.

Irene set down her tea cup on the side table and folded her hands in her lap.

"So, your father's coming to see us?"

"Yes, Gran, as soon as he's finished the project he's working on. Hopefully by then I'll have found a spot for the idea I was telling you about so he can size it up."

He rose from the table.

"I think I'll walk down to the beach. I could do with some salt in my lungs to clear out the London air."

****

Christa frowned as she read Sarah's text again then quickly replied. Being charming to dinner guests wasn't her idea of a fun way to spend an evening, but hopefully Sarah wasn't too sick and it was just for tonight.

She discarded her worn jeans and sleeveless T-shirt and replaced them with a skirt and white blouse. Thank goodness she'd been to the hairdresser earlier for a cut and the faded red color could now get away with being called highlights. Christa finished her transformation with red lipstick and grabbed her tote bag and keys.

She headed off down the street to find a taxi, her heels clicking on cobblestones.

****

Dan's phone buzzed as he walked along the beach. He read Sarah's message and cursed. He could've done with an early night but wouldn't let Vince down.

Back at the house he called to his aunt in the kitchen.

"I'm having a quick shower then heading over to Mordros Bay. Sarah's not well and needs help tonight with Vince away."

He hurried up the stairs and tossed aside his jeans and T-shirt. He knotted a blue tie and smoothed down his hair before a final check in the mirror. Hopefully Sarah wasn't too sick and would be back tomorrow. Being charming to people wasn't his thing.

****

Christa stood at the end of the bed and listened to Sarah's instructions.

"Welcome people and check their reservation in the book. Lead them to their table and give them menus. Polly and Jim are on tonight. They'll help with anything you're not sure of."

"No problem. You rest and just let us know if you need anything." Christa berated herself for doubting Sarah on the way here; the poor girl looked dreadful. She'd do what she could to help.

****

"What are you doing here?" Dan stood in the entrance hall and gaped. The elegant woman standing in front of him bore little resemblance to his Christa. Even her hair was tastefully cut and gently flipped at the ends with mere touches of gentle red lights.

"At a wild guess, I'd say the same as you." She ran her gaze down over his suit.

"Sarah told you she was sick and needed help, right?" She smirked and Dan's brain worked overtime.

"D'Amato. I'll wring his neck."

"You don't think Sarah came up with this

herself?" Christa asked and Dan threw her a pitying look.

"Come off it. This has Vince's hallmark running right through it." Dan looked around. "Where's Sarah now?"

"Upstairs in bed looking ill. If she isn't, her performance earlier deserved an Oscar."

"She'll wish she really was ill in a minute." Dan turned away, but Christa suddenly grabbed his arm.

"Think a minute. What do they want us to do?" She calmly returned his puzzled look. "They expect us to burst into Sarah's room and accuse her of deception. Then she'll calm us down, we'll end up laughing at what a clever trick it was, and be all over each other again. It's our turn to have some fun with them."

Dan stared right into her blue eyes.

"What have you got in mind?"

A mischievous smile tugged at the corners of her lips.

"We don't do anything. We do our job then go home at the end of the evening and say nothing."

Another four or five hours in close proximity to Christa would strain his powers of endurance and Dan wasn't sure he could survive it even to thwart Vince.

"I suppose it's as good an idea as any," he said grudgingly.

Christa smoothed down her skirt and Dan quickly walked away. He felt her smile on his back and knew he was in trouble.

****

Dan rubbed at his aching knee. Standing this long wasn't smart, but he was determined not to give in and sit down.

"Polly says for us to go ahead and leave. I told her we'd check in with Sarah tomorrow to make sure she's recovered." Christa popped up next to him, grinning like mad.

"It took her a second to remember Sarah's supposed to be ill. Boy, did she ever turn bright scarlet."

He struggled to force out a smile. He could hardly say goodnight and drive off without offering her a lift home.

"Uh, do you want a..."

"Don't worry about me. Molly's leaving soon and I'm going home with her."

"It's no trouble and it'll save her having to go out of her way to drop you off." He must be the world's stupidest man.

"OK, thanks. I'll go and tell Molly. Meet you in the car."

Dan lowered the windows and let in the cooling evening air. He was grateful for the warning of her footsteps crunching across the gravel, but the waft of her light floral scent forced him to suck in a deep breath. He gestured towards the windows.

"Is it too cold for you?"

"No, it feels good."

Neither spoke for ages and he drove slower than usual. Dan pulled into a parking spot near Robbie's shop and she finally broke the silence.

"Thanks."

"You're welcome." Dan wished she'd go before he said something stupid. "I don't suppose you fancy a drink?" Something exactly like that.

She studied him hard and he almost withdrew the offer.

"Are you sure?"

"Of course. I'll leave the car here if you're OK with walking."

She nodded and got out while Dan retrieved his cane from the back seat. She matched her pace to his as they walked down the road but didn't take his arm.

Their favourite corner table was free and Dan gratefully sat down and exhaled, the pain jabbing through his knee.

"Do you mind getting the drinks?" With Christa he didn't need to explain.

"No problem. I don't know about you but I'm starving. Do you want something?"

"I could manage a sandwich." He reached for his wallet but she shook her head.

"Put that away, it's my treat tonight. Will beer and a ham sandwich work for you?"

"Better make it a soda water and lime. I'll need a pill when I get home."

Five minutes and she was back. Christa unloaded the tray and their hands gently brushed together.

"Do you mind if I take my tie off?" He quickly removed it and grabbed a sandwich. At least eating might prevent him saying anything else stupid.

"After we're done , how about I take you back where you belong?" There, he'd said it.

"But you said…"

"It doesn't matter what I said. I was stupid, OK? All I need to know is whether it's what you want, too…"

The words stuck in his throat. Dan focused hard on Christa and waited.

Proposals And Protests

CHRISTA had to clear things up before they went any further.

"I'm not coming back and continuing to drift along with you. That's not enough."

A slow smile crept across Dan's face and something inside her warmed.

"I give in, all right? I can't say what I want to here. You mind if we leave now?"

She nodded and they stood up together. This time she slid her arm through his and they walked back to his car.

"How are we going to explain my coming back?"

"Perhaps by telling them the truth in the morning? Trust me – they'll be pleased I've finally done something sensible."

Dan gave her a quick peck on the cheek and unlocked the door. They crept into the kitchen and he pulled her into his arms.

"This isn't how I intended to say this." His words throbbed with emotion. "Nothing about us getting together has been conventional, so why start now?

"I love you, Christa. I've loved you since the day you stepped out on that train platform flinging your wild red hair around. We've a lot to sort out, but if you'll consider marrying me, I'll be the luckiest man on earth. And if we're lucky enough to be blessed with a child..." His breath hitched. "That'd be the most wonderful thing ever."

Christa was struck dumb at Dan's heartfelt words.

"Say something, for goodness' sake."

The frantic edge to his plea cut through her heart.

"Oh, Dan, I love you, too, and I want to say yes."

He cradled her trembling hands.

"Take your time, sweetheart. It's a big decision and in our case it's not straightforward, is it?

"If we're supposed to be together why am I considering it so sensibly?"

"It's not simple, sweetheart. Talk to your family, go and see them or bring them here. Take as long as you need." He sighed heavily. "Of course, I might go crazy waiting, but you'll have to take the chance."

Christa traced her fingers over his face, taking in every contour, each mark of life on his skin and wondered how it was possible to love someone so much.

"I won't make you wait any longer than I have to."

"I know you won't." He pressed his warm mouth against hers. "Now, I think it's bedtime and then in the morning we'll face the inquisition together."

"I think I'll let you do it alone," she teased.

"Not if you value your life, you won't."

****

Dan draped his arm around Christa's shoulder as they walked into the kitchen into the direct gaze of two pairs of eyes.

"Christa, what a nice surprise." Mary's mischievous smile said she'd heard them come in last night.

Dan could tell Mary and Gran were desperate to know what was going on, so he decided to put them out of their misery.

He grinned as he quickly explained about Sarah's deception and how he'd persuaded Christa to return. Then he floundered over how much else to share and stared helplessly at Christa.

Christa squeezed his hand and beamed a confident smile.

"We're back together again and making plans for the future, but they aren't settled yet. When they are, you'll be the first to know."

Irene jumped in to speak before her daughter had the chance.

"Well, I'll speak for us both and say we're some pleased. You're obviously meant to be together. It won't be easy, but you're old enough to know that."

Christa glanced shyly at Dan and his heart melted.

"If you haven't got anything special planned today I could do with your help. There are lots of details about Saturday's protest still left to sort."

He'd been planning to start searching for a possible property but no way would he turn down her offer.

"I'm all yours."

"Good." Christa's voice broke and he couldn't resist giving her a quick kiss.

Christa zipped through her checklist.

"A boatload of posters are up already. Flyers delivered to all the houses. The local TV and radio stations are lined up to cover the meeting." Christa couldn't suppress a large grin. "Best of all, your local MP's coming for support."

Dan whistled.

"How'd you manage that?"

"With a touch of my legendary charm naturally. OK…I'll concede I had some help. Marc Trelawney socialises with him occasionally and put in a word for us. I believe the mention of TV cameras helped."

Dan warm laugh tickled all the way through her.

"Great job. Did you say Ivan Carhart was wavering on supporting us?"

She nodded.

"Yeah, I didn't get the impression he'd stand up to his mother if it came to it."

"He said to keep in touch, though, didn't he? Why don't you set up a private meeting and I'll come with you, if you want. I've known him for ever because he was my maths tutor when Jonathan needed to get me up to speed before he sent me to boarding school."

"Why didn't you tell me before, you exasperating man?"

"I never thought to."

She thrust her mobile phone at him.

"Call. Set something up for today."

Dan threw a mock salute.

"Yes, ma'am."

Five minutes later, with a lunch date arranged, he had Christa back in his arms and was a happy man.

****

Ivan entered, nervously checking out the room, and Dan quickly stood to greet him before his old teacher could change his mind and leave.

"Good to see you and thanks for coming."

Dan kept the conversation light while they ordered from the menu and when their appetisers arrived gave Christa a discreet nod to take over.

"I hope you don't mind me calling you Ivan. I'm not one for standing on ceremony? Typical American, I guess."

Dan almost choked as she fluttered her eyelashes at the poor man.

"I know you're in an awkward position but sometimes we've got to stand up for what we believe in, don't we?" She fixed her most compelling gaze on him and Dan crossed his fingers under the table.

Ivan cleared his throat.

"Well, yes, but it's not easy."

She moved in closer and touched his arm.

"Nothing worthwhile ever is, Ivan."

"What exactly do you want me to do?" Ivan sounded resigned and Dan suppressed the urge to cheer.

"We're having a protest rally down on the quay this Saturday morning. Most of the villagers will be there, plus the local TV and radio stations and newspapers and Paul Westmorland, the MP."

Ivan went steadily paler as Christa went into more details.

"We'd love you to give your support. You wouldn't have to say anything." She flashed a bewitching smile. "Although if you want to that would be awesome."

He fiddled with his wine glass.

"Let me get this clear. You want me to

take part in a protest that'll be all over the local media against a business scheme that my brother's leading?"

"That about sums it up." Christa smiled broadly. "So are you with us or not?"

Dan wished she'd been more tactful. He got a grim feeling she'd pushed too hard.

A slow ghost of a smile inched its way across the other man's face.

"I believe I am. It'll burn my boats and I'll have to move out of the house, but that's long overdue. Brother or not, Pat's only ever cared about money."

He took a deep swallow of wine.

"Plus, the real reason he's selling the shops is unbelievably juvenile, isn't it?"

Dan and Christa exchanged confused glances.

"Oh, this is funny. You don't know, do you?" Ivan allowed Dan to refill his glass. "Pat was briefly married years ago, but his wife left him and now he's been turned down by Emma in the gift shop. He wooed her in his usual way and she told him she wasn't interested. This is his revenge."

Dan gave a long slow whistle.

"I didn't see that one coming. So he's going to ruin six families' livelihoods and rip out the heart of the village instead. Great."

"That about sums it up." Ivan jumped to his feet. "Anyway, thanks for lunch. I must be going before Mother asks too many questions. See you Saturday."

He left them both stunned into silence.

Family Matters

DON'T even think about it." Dan admonished Christa.

"What?" Her mind raced as she plotted her next move.

"You are not going to tackle Emma! Allow her to keep her dignity and leave quietly, the way she wants."

"OK. Well, how about we confront Pat Carhart instead? You don't think he might be overcome with guilt?" Christa played with the ends of her hair and pondered.

"No, you'll only make him more determined. Pat's proud , he'd hate it to be publicly known she turned him down."

"I give in then." She tossed her hands up in surrender. "Let's go back to the café and give them an update. After that, I'd better get my stuff from Robbie's."

"I'll come, too." Dan's voice made it clear he wasn't going to brook any argument.

"I don't think that's…"

He instantly pulled over the car and stopped, tenderly holding of her hands.

"Give in for once. Please."

The strong, feminist, side of her wanted to protest, but there was something comforting about Dan's protective side. In that instant it took all her self-control not to accept his marriage proposal on the spot. She planted a soft kiss on his lips.

Her voice was husky with emotion.

"I'll call my folks tonight and ask them to come over for a visit."

He grinned.

"I'll practise driving slower so I don't freak out your mother."

They parked outside Robbie's and Christa pushed open the door. Robbie glanced up.

"I came to pick up my things. I appreciated you letting me stay, but I'm moving back in with the Treneagues."

Christa hesitated a second but Dan's firm hand on her shoulder gave her strength.

"Dan and I have sorted things out."

"Fair enough. I hope things work out," Robbie said with a friendly smile. "On you go."

He turned to Dan.

"Would you like to see the old photos of the shops Penmount came up with?" He rifled around in the desk drawer and spread out a stack of black and white pictures.

Christa left them to it and it didn't take long before she was back downstairs and they had the car loaded. She sighed.

"Everyone's going to be at the house and I just need a little time alone with you."

"How about we pay another visit to Penwarren Woods?"

"That'd be perfect. Lead on, my hero."

Lying on a blanket on the sun-warmed grass while Dan dozed beside her Christa studied his face. Long dark lashes swept his tanned skin while his rich brown eyes closed in rest. She tenderly traced the sharp definition of his cheekbones.

She couldn't wait any longer.

"Wake up. I need to make a phone call." She shook Dan's shoulder. He stirred and rubbed his eyes.

"What's the hurry, sweetheart?"

"I've got to tell my parents you'd make a wonderful son-in-law."

Dan pressed his finger to her lips.

"I understand. Your family is important to you. Mine are to me, too, but they already love you so I've got it easy."

"Your father hasn't met me." Christa couldn't wait to meet Jonathan Wilson.

"No, but I'm not worried. He's got good taste. Like me."

****

Christa checked her appearance; a smart black linen skirt and yellow shirt, suitably striking for television.

Her mother's voice replayed in her head for the millionth time. Forty-eight hours after they spoke every word replayed in her mind; the questions, the concerns and the pleas not to do anything hasty.

A bang on the door shook her from her thoughts.

"Are you ready? We need to get going." Dan strode in as he fitted a green beret closely to his head.

The sharply tailored lovat green dress uniform, rows of medal ribbons, and polished black boots stunned her.

"What's with all the impressive gear?" Dan shrugged.

"I wouldn't usually resort to this, but we need all the support we can get and it attracts attention, especially with the cane."

"Warn me next time so I can still my fluttering heart." Christa didn't want him to guess how disconcerted he'd made her.

She grabbed her bag and swiftly headed for the door.

* * * *

Christa turned the corner and stopped short – silenced by the sight of around a thousand people gathered around the quay. Tears pushed against her eyes and she appreciated the weight of Dan's hand on her shoulder.

"Better than expected?"

"You could say that."

Posters were on every available wall and people waved home-made protest banners.

Christa and Dan pushed their way towards the stage in the middle of the street. She noticed Dan flinch as TV cameras flashed in his face and he struggled to smile.

"He's here." Dan pointed to Ivan Carhart. "Westmorland's nabbed him, so Ivan's cornered. You need to get over there." He gave Christa a gentle push, but she grabbed his hand and pulled him along to join her.

Christa's speech got a rousing reception then Ivan grabbed the microphone from her hands and spoke out vehemently against his brother's plans. Christa hoped his mother would see this on television and not be so quick to condemn her youngest son.

Pat Carhart was nowhere in sight but they hadn't expected him to show his face. No doubt he had an appointed spy among the crowd to report back.

An hour later the crowd started to disperse into the pubs and cafés. Christa was on a high, knowing that even if Carhart went through with his plans no-one would forget they'd tried.

A hand touched her back and she started.

"I might've guessed my girl would be in the centre of things, causing trouble again."

Walt Reynolds seized her by the shoulders and planted a large kiss on her cheek.

"Couldn't you leave Cornwall in peace?"

"When did you get here, and where's Mom?" Christa spun around, searching for her mother.

Suzie whirled her daughter into a hug.

"I'm here, you meddling creature! How have you managed to disrupt a whole village in a few weeks?"

"With charm and persuasion."

Dan's crisp voice broke through as he limped over to join them, so handsome Christa's heart swelled with pride. He held out his hand to Christa's father and introduced himself before turning to do the same to her mother. She'd take a guess he hadn't been this scared since Afghanistan.

"That sounds like our girl."

"I can't believe you guys flew in without telling me?" Christa couldn't get her head around the fact they were here.

"Yep, we arrived yesterday and crashed at a hotel then got the overnight train down. Don't even know what day it is."

Walt roared with laughter.

"Charming place, this. I can see why you don't want to leave."

"I didn't say..." Her voice trailed away

and Christa smiled up at Dan, completely out of words and in need of rescue.

"I need to go and change out of these hot clothes. Can't believe I used to tolerate hours on the parade ground in all this gear. If you don't have any other plans how about we have dinner together tonight?"

"Better make it lunch or we'll be too tired to string two words together," her father answered. "Christa can show us around and meet you at the house, if that suits you. Suzie's bursting to meet the family."

"That'd be fine, sir. Get her to take you to the café. My aunt and gran are there serving up tea and gossip if I know them."

He leaned in and gave Christa a kiss.

"See you at home, I'll ring Vince to get a table," he whispered in her ear.

Christa and her parents found a quiet spot to sit overlooking the sparkling sea.

"That's quite a man you've found. Do you think you're up to it?" her mother asked and her father's brow furrowed with a mixture of tiredness and worry.

"Shouldn't we ask if he is?"

Christa rushed to Dan's defense.

"In what way? If you're referring to his bad knee it's not a big deal. Sure, he can't do some things, but he's still got lots going for him." She crossed her arms and glared.

"He loves me and he's the most

honorable man I've ever met."

"We're concerned about you making long term plans with Dan so quickly." She smiled. "But we can't say much, as we met and married within six weeks ourselves."

Christa put an arm around them both.

"If we're half as happy as you two we'll be blessed. We'd better go because Aunt Mary and Granny Irene will have heard you're here and be dying to meet you."

It was a struggle to escape without eating the food the Treneague women tried to press on them. Suzie made plans to get together with Irene later to look at photos and talk about her mother as a young girl.

As her parents were leaving, Christa opened the front door, to come face to face with an unknown man, smiling at her. Her eyes swept over the man – an older version of Dan with startling blue eyes and immaculate silver blond hair.

"Jonathan Wilson. We meet at last."

An Amazing Announcement

HELLO. I often accuse Dan of exaggerating, but not on this occasion. A beauty indeed."

Christa flushed with pleasure and Jonathan immediately switched his attention to her awestruck parents.

"You must be Mr and Mrs Reynolds?"

"Walt and Suzie, please, we're too tired to stand on ceremony."

Dan suddenly appeared by Christa's side.

"Dad! Why didn't you tell us you were coming?"

"Thought I'd surprise you!" Jonathan smiled.

"Well, you're just in time. Aunt Mary and Gran are working at the café, but the rest of us have a table booked at Mordros Bay for half past one. You'll join us, of course?"

"Glad to!" Jonathan grinned.

Dan greeted Vince with a sigh of relief, not seeing their families in sight.

"They're on their second drinks so they should be relaxed. I told them your car's slow."

Dan snatched Christa's hand and steered her firmly towards the bar where they found Jonathan holding court.

"Come on, son, we're all starving, tell

your friend, Vince, we're ready to order – and before you argue I intend sitting next to your charming young lady."

His expression told Dan not to argue and to work on Christa's parents while he had the chance.

Dan did as he was told. The combination of amazing food and a killer view didn't hurt his case, and by the time dessert arrived he managed to relax. Christa's full, throaty laugh rang out and he glanced over to see her enjoying one of Jonathan's jokes.

Out of the blue, Vince appeared at his elbow and whispered in Dan's ear. His heart sank and he glanced warily towards the door.

"Sorry to interrupt your lunch." Pat Carhart glared defiantly around at them all.

"Remember what I said." Emma fidgeted beside him, looking awkward.

Dan stood up and worked hard to hold on to his temper.

"This isn't the place, Mr Carhart. Could we talk later?"

"No, we can't. I want this over with." Emma interrupted.

"What he means to say is that he has some good news, don't you, Pat?"

He shuffled his feet and glanced down at the floor.

"Yes. I'm not much for speeches."

"Really. We hadn't noticed." Christa appeared by his side and Dan took hold of her hand.

"I've given it some thought, and talked to my family and Miss Tregorick here..." A slight tinge of colour lit up his cheeks. "I acted hastily over the shops." He cleared his throat and turned a deeper shade of pink. "I've told the developers I've changed my mind and I'm not selling. We'll draw up new leases and carry on as we were."

Pat turned to walk away, but Emma's firm hand on his elbow held him in place.

"If everyone's happy with that, of course," he mumbled.

Dan pulled himself together, still in shock and unsure how to reply.

"We appreciate you rethinking things. We'll pass this on to the others and be in touch. I'm sure they'll be in agreement."

Christa's hand tensed in his, but he was determined not to make things too easy for the other man. He fixed his attention on Emma instead and smiled.

"Thank you." Their eyes met and she gave a brief nod. Some things were better left unsaid.

Everyone around the table stayed quiet until the couple left.

"We did it! We did it!" Christa punched a hand in the air, her yell startling the other diners. She flung her arms around Dan's neck and kissed him, tears coursing down her face.

Reluctant to stifle her exuberance, he held on tight and threw a helpless smile at their confused families.

"Sweetheart, why don't you sit down? Maybe Vince can arrange for some coffee and we'll explain what's going on." Dan eased her into the chair next to him and kept an arm around her shoulder. He gave a brief rundown and fielded questions while Christa bubbled over with excitement.

Christa's mother yawned and apologised.

"I'm exhausted. I thought Cornwall was supposed to be a quiet backwater but it doesn't seem like it to me. I'm sure you two want to pass this news around so maybe Jonathan can give us a lift to our hotel?"

"I'd be happy to." He turned to Dan. "I'll be at the house later. Once you've got this sorted I want to nail you down on the other project. I've only got a couple of days free."

"You're a hard taskmaster. Never a wasted minute, eh?" Their comfortable agreement made Dan's throat tighten. It'd been too long since things between them were this way.

"That's right, my boy. Tomorrow morning we're off to look at properties."

Dan started to protest.

"But I haven't had time to…"

"I realise that, and maybe I shouldn't have interfered, but you asked for my help so I checked out a few possibilities from London and we're viewing five places tomorrow."

Dan gave in.

"Are you doing anything tomorrow, love?" he asked Christa.

Mixed emotions crossed her face and he guessed he should've been more thoughtful, but then her mother spoke up.

"It's all right. You go with Dan. I've planned to meet Irene to swap photos and hear her wartime stories. How about we have dinner together in the evening? Maybe you can take us to a real pub."

"We sure can, but you have to let us order for you." She grinned at Dan as they both pictured Suzie tackling a loaded plate of scampi and chips.

In a flurry of goodbyes Jonathan whisked the couple away, leaving Dan and Christa still trying to come to terms with everything that had happened.

"Wow, who'd have expected that?"

"Not me. What made him change his mind?"

"Maybe Emma? I'm just glad he did." Christa stated firmly. "Let's go and see everyone at the shops."

The village grapevine had worked

overtime. One phone call from Molly Pendean who'd overheard Pat Carhart making his announcement and Christa and Dan walked right into a welcoming crowd.

In the middle of everything they caught sight of Robbie, quietly leaning against his shop doorway.

"I need to thank him. He was a good friend when I needed one," Christa insisted and Dan knew she was right.

"Congratulations. You must be pleased." Robbie smiled at Christa.

"You were a huge help. Getting Ivan Carhart to come through for us definitely played an important part."

"Something else was his doing, too, wasn't it, you interfering young creature?"

Emma Tregorick walked into the shop, her eyes twinkling.

"I bet he hasn't told you." She brushed off Robbie's attempt to shush her. "I'd no idea why Pat Carhart was causing all this trouble until my neighbour couldn't keep his mouth shut."

"But how did you know, Robbie?" Christa was confused and watched him squirm. "You saw Ivan again?"

"He happened to come in the pub after the protest and I bought him a drink – several actually. It wasn't hard to get him to share the story of his own accord."

Robbie flashed a disarming grin.

"I took a guess you'd have too many scruples to use the information, but I didn't." An easy shrug explained away his logic. "I thought Emma deserved to be told and then the rest was her choice."

He put an arm around Emma's shoulder.

"She did well, is all I'm saying." Robbie planted a kiss on her cheek.

"She certainly did." Dan's deep voice interjected. "And so did you."

Christa cautiously touched Emma's arm. "Do you still plan to leave your shop?"

"Yes, my dear. My sister's not well so I'm going to live with her to help out for a while. She's got a little shop, too, so we'll work it together, but I'll be back to visit. Pat's insisting on coming to Torquay and bringing me down sometimes for the day."

Christa struggled for the right thing to say, completely at a loss as to what this quiet, soft-spoken woman saw in the brash businessman.

"That's good news. Make sure you come by and see us all," Dan told her, when no-one else spoke up.

"Pat's a kind man underneath all that bluster. Some people cover up shyness by being rude," Emma said.

"I'm sure you're right and let us know if you need any help moving." Dan grabbed

Christa's hand. "We must be off now."

Back at the house, they went straight into the kitchen. Dan turned the kettle on and flashed Christa a quick smile.

"Don't know about you, but I need a cup of tea and a few minutes to take all this in. It's been quite a day."

She caught Dan's eye and smiled slowly. He'd guessed she needed space to think.

"We're home," Aunt Mary called out from the hall and Dan groaned.

"Should've guessed we wouldn't get a minute to ourselves."

Christa smiled at his rueful grin, knowing he loved his family as much as she did hers.

"Right, time for tea, you pair. Off you go in the other room with Gran and I'll bring it in when I've got it all ready."

Doing what they were told was the easiest way.

"There we go. I thought we deserved chocolate cake tonight. You, young woman, deserve a whole cake to yourself after what you've done."

Mary settled the tray on the table and began to pass teacups around.

The front door slammed and Jonathan strolled in.

"Did I hear those most wonderful of words – chocolate cake – spoken by my favorite cook?"

He beamed and gave Mary a warm kiss on her cheek.

Setting down his plate, Jonathan glanced over at Dan.

"If you're free, how about going through those property listings? Perhaps we can go in the other room?"

"Are you coming?" Dan held out a hand to Christa and she felt absurdly pleased.

On the dining-room table Jonathan spread out the papers.

Dan grabbed one, his eyes gleaming with barely suppressed excitement.

"This is it, I'll bet money on it. Let's see this one first, if we can."

Jonathan grinned.

"Nine o'clock, already arranged."

****

To Dan it wasn't an abandoned holiday camp, but a place with great potential.

There was space and peace, exactly what he'd craved after his injury but hadn't been able to find.

He scanned the broken-down cabins and empty swimming pool and decided it was no wonder this place went out of business. Miles from any shops or entertainment it wouldn't have suited normal holidaymakers. But his guests wouldn't be the ordinary kind and for them its isolation was perfect. He wandered around, making notes.

Loud laughter interrupted his thoughts and he turned to see Christa and his father chatting happily together. She popped a kiss on Jonathan's cheek then ran to join him.

"Your father's being nosey."

"I bet you put him in his place." He swooped down for a brief kiss, relishing the warmth of her soft lips.

"Come and see." Dan took her hand and led her off towards the dilapidated building. "Can you see it? We'll rip this down and build a new centre," he told her excitedly. "This'll be for classrooms, therapy, a cinema, dining-room, that kind of thing. The interior needs to be very simple – all clean lines, pale colours, and no fuss."

Dan stopped.

"What time are we meeting your parents?" His hands moved to rest on her shoulders.

"Seven. Jonathan's bringing them down to meet us at the Bosun's."

"I thought we'd ask Auntie Mary and Gran to join us?" His casual voice was betrayed by a slight tremor.

"Have you got something important to tell them?"

A chill of anticipation ran through Dan and he went very still.

"I don't know, do I?"

"I've been thinking, and you know what conclusion I've come to?" If she kept him waiting much longer he'd be tempted to shake her. "I love you and you love me. I want to spend the rest of my life with you and I'm pretty sure you're inclined to do the same. I've thought about it a bunch. I'll miss my family but I want to settle here and help you with all this."

She gestured around them.

"So, yes – I'll marry you. You still want to, don't you?" Her voice shook.

"Oh, yes! I wasn't sure you'd…"

She touched his face and wiped away tears he wasn't aware were falling, and then he did the same to her in return.

"What a pair we are. This is supposed to be a happy moment and look at us."

Dan's voice thickened.

"I'd like to tell them all together, but…" An awful thought occurred to him. "They'll be looking for a ring and I don't have one."

Christa giggled helplessly.

"Oh, well, that's it, it's all off. No ring. No engagement." She gave Dan a not-so-gentle poke in the ribs. "You didn't think for a minute I'd let you choose it alone! This is something I intend to wear for the rest of my life. We'll choose it together."

He entwined his hand with hers and they walked slowly back towards his father.

"Don't say anything, either of you," Jonathan interjected, "I might be able to guess, but keep it until we're all together." A huge smile creased his face. "If I am right, I couldn't be happier. Now, much as you don't want to, we're still going to see the other properties. You might see one you like better and it's never wise to show too much interest in one before you start negotiating."

"But what's the point?" Dan protested.

His father shook his head.

"Haven't I taught you anything? If you're going to be a businessman you've got to behave like one."

"He's right," Christa agreed. "You want the best for your clients." She gave him a challenging glance and strode off.

Jonathan draped an arm around his son's shoulder.

"You might as well admit you're doomed. I envy you." His voice roughened and he walked quickly away towards his car.

His father hated showing any signs of weakness or lack of control so Dan held his tongue. For years he'd believed Jonathan led a charmed existence, but recently he'd seen how lonely the core of his life was. That wasn't how Dan wanted to live, and thanks to Christa he wouldn't have to.

He'd dutifully check out the other properties before facing the hardest part of the day and persuading Christa's parents he was the right man for her. No-one could love her more than he did and in the end it had to be what mattered.

"Come on, slowcoach," she called out, a brilliant smile lighting up her face.

"All right, woman!" Dan grinned and made his way over to the car.

****

"I guessed I'd find you here." Christa sat down next to her father on the Treneague's garden bench.

Since Dan's announcement in the pub he'd been very quiet. He studied her face, maybe trying to work out what his only daughter was thinking.

"Your mother's worried." Walt picked up her hand.

"And you aren't?" Christa's mouth twitched as she tried not to smile.

"Not really. Dan's a fine man and I trust him to care for you. I'll miss you being around as much." Walt cleared his throat. "It's not that your mother doesn't like him."

"That's OK. Moms are supposed to worry more, it goes with the territory."

Christa dropped her head to her father's shoulder.

"I suppose so. We'd better go back in,

pumpkin. I need to get my woman to bed before she drops. By tomorrow she'll be talking wedding plans, so you'd better have your answers ready or she'll take over."

"Thanks, Daddy." Her voice cracked and a single tear crept down her cheek.

Walt nodded, stood up, and strode off, almost marching down the garden path and Christa had to let him go.

Dan looked up from the kitchen table as Walt came in.

"She needs you." Walt smiled at his future son-in-law.

"I'll go to her. Don't think I'm trying to rush you off, but Suzie's eyes were fighting to stay open a few minutes ago. Jonathan will give you a lift whenever you like."

"Thanks, son. We'll see you tomorrow. I'm sure they'll be on to dress colours and flowers by then. My only advice is to agree to it all and offer no opinion whatsoever."

"I can do that." Dan touched the other man's shoulder. "Thanks for everything."

Dan joined her in the garden, slid his arms around her and absorbed her sobs into his broad chest. In a few minutes her tears lessened so he risked giving her a soft kiss.

"Let's go in. It's been a long day."

Christa's beautiful face lit up and she twined her arms around his neck.

"That's better. I love you."

"I love you, too, my angel."

He couldn't think of a better way of ending a day.

****

The Mordros Bay hotel twinkled with thousands of Christmas lights and music drifted out into the chilly night air. A crowd of noisy guests spilled out of the front door, drinks in hand, ready to send off the bride and groom.

Dan maneuvered Christa into the waiting white Rolls-Royce, its satin ribbons fluttering in the light. She pulled handfuls of confetti from her dress and shook out her hair sending a shower of coloured paper all over the car.

The last six months had exhausted every avenue of patience they possessed. By the time they'd dealt with immigration regulations, wedding plans, and begun to transform a derelict camp into a top notch rehab facility – this day often felt like it would never come. But here they were. The wedding had gone off without a hitch and "The Haven" would be open in the spring.

She took hold of Dan's left hand, smoothing her finger over the gold ring she'd placed there a few hours before.

"It certainly does, Mr Wilson."

Christa slid her hand up to cradle his face. "I'm a lucky woman."

She'd kissed a lot of frogs in her time, but a prince had been waiting and she'd only had to travel 4,000 miles to find him. Hers had turned out to be a real live version of the amber-eyed Cornish pisky she'd finally given him as a wedding gift.

The End

DC Thomson

Published in Great Britain by D.C. Thomson & Co., Ltd., Dundee, Glasgow and London. Distributed by Marketforce, Blue Fin Building, 110 Southwark Street, London SE1 0SU. Tel: +44 (0) 20 3148 3300. Fax: +44 (0) 20 3148 8105.
Website: www.marketforce.co.uk
© D.C. Thomson & Co., Ltd., and Angela Britnell, 2014

Don't miss the next Pocket Novel No. 755,
On sale April 24, 2014.

If you are looking for back numbers please telephone 0800 318846
Printed and bound by CPI Group (UK) Ltd., Croydon, CR0 4YY